# The Checkered Years

*Mary Dodge Woodward*

# The Checkered Years

## A Bonanza Farm Diary
## 1884–88

### MARY DODGE WOODWARD

EDITED BY
MARY BOYNTON COWDREY

WITH A NEW INTRODUCTION BY
ELIZABETH JAMESON

MINNESOTA HISTORICAL SOCIETY PRESS

www.mhspress.org

The Minnesota Historical Society Press
is a member of the Association of American University Presses.

10 9 8 7 6 5 4 3

∞ The paper used in this publication meets the minimum requirements of
the American National Standard for Information Sciences—Permanence for
Printed Library Materials, ANSI Z39.48-1984.

International Standard Book Number 0-87351-237-5 (paper)

*Library of Congress Cataloging-in-Publication Data*
Woodward, Mary Dodge, 1826–1890.
  The checkered years : a bonanza farm diary, 1884–88 / Mary Dodge
Woodward ; edited by Mary Boynton Cowdrey ; with an introduction by
Elizabeth A. Jameson.
     p. cm—(Borealis Books)
  Reprint. Originally published: Caldwell, Idaho : Caxton Printers, 1937.
  ISBN 0–87351–237–5
  1. Frontier and pioneer life—North Dakota.   2. Farm life—North
Dakota.   3. Woodward, Mary Dodge, 1826–1890—Diaries.
4. Farmers' wives—North Dakota—Diaries.   I. Cowdrey, Mary
Boynton, b. 1891.   II. Title.
F636.W66 1989
978.4'02'0924—dc 19                                                89-30974
[13]                                                                        CIP

# TABLE OF CONTENTS

*Page*

God made man in the East,
And let him travel West.

It is there our stake is driven,
In the Great Banana Belt.

The chinchbug eats the farmer's grain,
The bee-moth eats his honey.

The grain pours down in golden treasure,
With flow unchecked and rounded measure.

How strange it seems,
This changing of dates!

# LIST OF ILLUSTRATIONS

# INTRODUCTION TO
# THE REPRINT EDITION

MARY DODGE WOODWARD'S personal record of her life on a Dakota Territory "bonanza farm" adds new detail and texture to the histories of both women and the West. Her daily chronicle provides a perspective that is not part of our common historical understanding – that of a widow in her fifties and sixties who came west, not for adventure or personal gain, but to live with her unmarried children while her son managed a large commercial wheat farm.

Woodward's experience was not the West of popular myth and imagination, usually told through the heroic adventures of trappers, cowboys, prospectors, soldiers, or outlaws – mostly male, mostly young, mostly Anglo-American, mostly "unfettered" by family or communal ties. Women, if they had any part in this saga, appeared in minor, supporting roles, as one-dimensional caricatures. One stereotype of western women was the "reluctant pioneer," who, unfit for the rigors of western life, pining for the amenities of eastern culture, civilized the West, ending the men's rowdy good times. Another stereotype was the helpmate, who performed endless, oppressive labor as she "stood by her man." Then there were the "bad" women of the West, colorful renegades like Calamity Jane and Annie Oakley, or "whores with hearts of gold," who bore little resemblance to the real prostitutes and dance-hall women who lived and worked in cattle, lumber, mining, railroad, and garrison towns.[1] Good *or* bad, refined *or* hardworking, all young, almost all White, the mythic figures of western drama distort our history.

The story of the "real" West was much more human

and varied. It involved the painstaking daily work of establishing homes, farms, and communities, work in which real women with real strengths and weaknesses were central actors. Land drew most new settlers to the Dakota plains of Woodward's story. Single, married, and widowed, with and without men, women came west – for adventure, for economic gain, for a fresh start, often with mixed feelings about what they left and what they hoped to find.[2]

They worked hard. Sometimes they did fieldwork; more often they did traditional "women's work," growing vegetables, keeping poultry and other livestock, milking cows, making butter, preserving food, clothing their families, hauling water and heating it for laundry and bathing, and bearing and caring for children. Housecleaning itself was a challenge in poorly sealed homes with dirt floors or sod walls and without running water. Women earned money by selling products, like butter and eggs, or by performing services, like teaching, sewing, doing laundry, or keeping boarders. Moving beyond their households, they established a rich web of associations and institutions that knit communities together – friendship and kin networks, schools, churches, libraries, and clubs. They also used their organizing skills for self-empowerment, working for woman suffrage in the new states and territories. By 1914 women could vote in the territory of Alaska and eleven states, all of which, except Illinois, were west of the Mississippi River.[3]

Although most of these women were married, a large number of single women and widows established independent homesteads. The Homestead Act of 1862 enabled unmarried women as well as men to acquire 160 acres if they lived on the land and cultivated it for five years. According to land office records in Lamar, Colorado, and Douglas, Wyoming, for 1887, 1891, 1907, and 1908, an average 11.9 percent of new homesteaders were women. More women than men proved up and obtained title to their land – 42.4 percent of the women as compared with 37 percent of the men.[4] *The Checkered Years* suggests yet another side of western widowhood. Mary Dodge Woodward was the principal homemaker and domestic manager for her family and for the extensive work crews employed in large-scale agriculture.

The story of women who established homesteads and communities helps to create a more accurate picture of the West. *The Checkered Years* adds much to that picture. The least accessible history is the common intimate detail of daily private and personal experience. That is what Mary Dodge Woodward recorded in the diaries that were an annual New Year's present from her son. She wrote for herself, with no thought of publication. Her diary, she said, was "a great deal of company," an "old friend," in which she recorded "blots, mistakes, joys, and sorrows." She wrote every day and compared her handwriting to the textures of the quilts she stitched. "My writing resembles feather-stitching and French knots," she commented.[5] Each entry is similar to a quilt square, a textured fragment of the writer and her world. The checkered patchwork of memory and reflection, of daily acts and observations, conveys a full range of emotion and experience. It is not the stereotypical portrait of a reluctant pioneer or romantic adventurer, but a fully dimensional expression of comfort and loneliness, beauty and pain, accomplishment and loss. The "checkered years" (a reference to Phoebe Cary's poem, "Old Pictures") held, in Woodward's words, "joy and woe . . . dark and light . . . rose and thorn." She called her quilts "comfortables," and she seemed, if not always happy, comfortable with all the pieces of her life.[6]

Woodward recorded both experience and memory, contrasts of youth and age, of old homes in Vermont and Wisconsin and the new home near Fargo. The comparisons were not stark. She was not an elderly woman romanticizing her youth or idealizing her old home in the East. Fully engaged in the present, Woodward also appreciated her past and missed some of the people who had shared it. Her diary became a substitute for the husband and neighbors she had lost.

She recorded the end of her life, but not the end of her living. Woodward and three of her children spent more than six years, from the fall of 1882 until the spring of 1889, on her cousin's Dakota farm. Mary Dodge Woodward died a year and a half later, on Christmas Day, 1890, in her old home in Kingston, Wisconsin. She was sixty-four. Almost half a century later her granddaughter, Mary Boynton Cowdrey, edited the diaries and published them. *The Checkered Years* appeared in 1937.

We know little of Woodward's life beyond the five-year record she left. Like many "ordinary" people, she left few documents from which to reconstruct her biography. Born in Vermont on June 27, 1826, she was the third of five daughters of Joel and Sabra Salisbury Dodge. Joel Dodge was an ironmaker who, his great-granddaughter cryptically reported, was "unfortunate and improvident as had been his father before him." Mary Dodge was eight years old when her mother died, and the five little girls were "parceled out" to relatives.[7] Mary went to live with a great-uncle, John Dodge, on his Vermont farm. Years later, his son Daniel (the "cousin Daniel" of *The Checkered Years*) brought her to Dakota.

Mary Dodge married another Vermonter, John Perkins Woodward, in Rutland, Vermont, on August 22, 1847. She was twenty-one; he, twenty-five. The Woodwards' first child, Theron Royal, was born May 25, 1848. He was followed on March 23, 1851, by a daughter, Julia (called Nellie), and by Walter Beach Woodward, born November 26, 1852.[8]

The great-uncle with whom Mary Dodge lived as a child was a cousin of Henry Dodge, the first territorial governor of Wisconsin. Whether because of that family connection or for other reasons, the Woodwards left Rutland on April 2, 1855, and moved to Kingston, Green Lake County, Wisconsin. Mary Woodward's father ("Gramp" of the diaries) accompanied them, and all of Mary Dodge Woodward's sisters eventually settled there.[9]

Serial family migration was common, and a pioneer journey might as often reunite a family as separate kin. Isabinda, the second of the Dodge sisters, married Walter Beach of Hinesburg, Vermont, in 1845. They moved to Wisconsin sometime between 1849 and 1851.[10] Lucy, the fourth of the sisters, was married in 1850 to Patrick Walsh, a Kingston merchant and lawyer, and the Walsh's five children were all born in Kingston. The youngest of the Dodge children, Martha Ann, married Lucius Warner of Rutland, Vermont, in 1852 but was widowed the following year. Left with an eight-month-old daughter, she apparently joined her family and in 1858 married Charles Goss, a merchant from Portage, Wisconsin. Their four children were all born in Kingston. Mary Woodward's oldest sister, Rachel Thayer, moved to Wisconsin sometime after 1853 (when the youngest of her three children was born in Vermont) and died in Kingston in 1879.[11]

Kingston was Mary Dodge Woodward's home for twenty-seven years. It held memories of her husband, children, and entire extended family. Yet we know only the barest outline of her years there. Her son Theron wrote a genealogy of the Dodge family. Beneath his mother's name, he wrote that John Woodward "held most of the offices in the gift of his town, and was almost continuously in office for nearly twenty-five years." He was "physically frail," having only one lung, and was therefore rejected for service in the Civil War. His son called him "a man of powerful intellect, an extensive reader and deep thinker." But of Mary Dodge Woodward herself, Theron wrote nothing.[12]

When John Woodward died in 1879, he was justice of the peace, conveyancer, and pension agent. An 1869 Kingston directory listed him as a shoemaker. Beyond these few facts and the fond references in his widow's diaries, we know little of him or of the family's fortunes. There is no trace of the "old brown house" frequently mentioned in *The Checkered Years* on plats or maps of Green Lake County for 1857, 1860, or 1875. Indeed, the only property attributed to any of the extended family in the few surviving records was forty acres that belonged to "P. Walsh" in 1875.[13]

Like many nineteenth-century women, Mary Dodge Woodward spent much of her life bearing and raising children. She had the first when she was not quite twenty-two, the last at thirty-eight. The youngest three were born after the move to Kingston. Kate arrived on April 3, 1859, and Fred Dodge on December 20, 1864. Between them came Gertrude, who lived less than a month, from November 20 to December 7, 1863. The Woodward children ranged in age from fourteen to thirty-one when their father died on November 26, 1879. It was Walter's twenty-seventh birthday.[14]

After her husband's death, Thanksgiving was a hard

time for Mary Woodward, and holidays in Dakota inevitably triggered memories of earlier and happier celebrations. She came to "almost dread the day" and wrote "I always feel more lonely at this time of year." Thanksgiving Day, 1878, was the last the family spent together, and never after their father's death were all the children with their mother for the holiday.[15]

The two eldest children were married. John Woodward performed the ceremony when Nellie married Elmore George Boynton, a merchant and manufacturer of Portage, Wisconsin, on October 2, 1874. Theron had already left home. He "entered the transportation business" in Chicago in 1869, and in 1877 married Anna Elizabeth Stevens, a Kingston native. They had two children, Harriet Valentine, born May 15, 1878, and Mortimer Stevens, born November 9, 1879, the "two good grandchildren" who appear in *The Checkered Years*. At some point Theron moved to Kansas City and became a journalist, working on the Kansas City *Daily Times*. In August 1883 Anna Woodward died, and Nellie took the two children to raise.[16]

After John Woodward died, Walter seems to have taken financial responsibility for the family. He was town clerk of Kingston and, like his father, held many local offices. In 1882 his mother's cousin, Daniel Dodge, offered him one thousand dollars a year and expenses to manage his fifteen-hundred-acre farm near Fargo in the Red River Valley of the North, and on October 18, Mary Dodge Woodward and her three youngest children settled on the Dodge farm. Two years later she wrote, "I have enjoyed my life here very much and have never wished to leave." She had "plenty to do." "But then," she wrote, "we are here to work."[17]

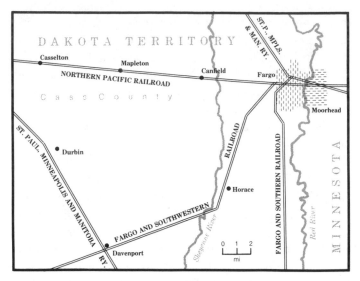

*From the Dodge farm, situated in the middle of a triangle formed by rail lines, Mary Woodward could look east across the Sheyenne River to see the lights of Fargo.*

By the late eighteenth century, fur traders had visited the Red River Valley of the North. Some had settled there and married Ojibway (Chippewa) and Dakota (Sioux) women, adding their Métis children to the English, French, and American Indian cultures of the area. A number of Métis and a few Europeans established the Pembina settlement in the 1820s.[18]

Significant settlement by Euro-Americans, however, did not occur until the post-Civil War boom encouraged by railroads and by new farming and milling technologies. The Red River valley became an important trade route to Canada because transportation costs from St. Paul were less than shipping via Hudson Bay. In 1869 the Dominion of Canada organized the province of Manitoba and opened it to settlement. The fact that Ottawa did not consult the residents of the area about the administrative change was partly responsible for the 1869 rebellion of Métis led by Louis Riel, to whom Woodward referred in her diaries.[19] Through the 1870s there was considerable migration from Ontario, increased steamboating on the Red River, the beginning of a railroad from St. Paul to Winnipeg, and agricultural settlement of eastern North Dakota.[20]

To finance railway construction in the United States after the Civil War, individual states and the federal government gave railroads enormous grants of public land for each mile of track completed, more than 129 million acres altogether.[21] The railroad grants, at least as much as the Homestead Act, brought settlers west and were instrumental in the development of the Red River valley of *The Checkered Years.*

The first railroad actually built within North Dakota was the Northern Pacific, which Congress chartered in 1864 and gave 50 million acres to build from Duluth to Puget Sound. The railroad received twenty sections per mile on alternate sides of the track in the states (Minnesota and Oregon), and forty sections per mile in the territories (Dakota, Montana, Idaho, and Washington). This amounted to more than six thousand square miles of land across Dakota, or roughly the area of Rhode Island and Connecticut combined. Construction westward from Lake Superior began in 1870. The railroad reached the Red River at Moorhead, Minnesota, in late 1871, crossed a new bridge over the river in June 1872, and arrived at Bismarck a year later.[22]

Of the billion acres of public land available in the United States when the Homestead Act was passed in 1862, about half was in private hands by 1900, but only 10 to 12 percent was distributed free under the act.[23] Some North Dakotans received land by improving it under the terms of the Homestead Act or the Timber Culture Act of 1873, which offered 160 acres to persons who planted ten of those acres in trees, but most purchased their property. They bought land from the Northern Pacific Railroad or from the federal government under the Pre-emption Act. Anyone who owned less than 320 acres in the United States or its territories could buy 160 acres for $1.25 an acre, or $2.50 on the government sections that alternated with the railroad's along the right-of-way. Before buying, the settler had to live on the land six months and make improvements. Homesteaders, too, could buy their land under the terms specified in the Pre-emption Act.

By 1890 the citizens of the new state of North Dakota had purchased more than 8 million acres – 4.6 million from the government and 3.5 million from the Northern Pacific. They had proved up on another 3.6 million acres but had abandoned 5.3 million acres. Many simply left. Some found the going too rough; others bought land for speculation and never intended to stay.[24]

The Northern Pacific and other railroads used their land as security with investors. Preferred stocks and bonds could be exchanged at face value for railroad lands.[25] Among those who invested in the Northern Pacific was Daniel Dodge, who had become wealthy through his invention of a machine for manufacturing horseshoe nails.

Jay Cooke, the prominent Philadelphia banker, launched an extensive campaign to sell $100 million worth of bonds, emphasizing the commercial potential of the "Fertile Belt" through which the railroad would run, but he could not raise funds as quickly as the Northern Pacific spent them. The resulting personal and company bankruptcies precipitated the national economic panic, or depression, of 1873–77.[26]

For western land speculators, the situation was a boon. Northern Pacific preferred stock with a paper value of $100 sold for $14, which meant it was worth seven times its market value if exchanged for railroad land because land was selling at $2.50 to $5 an acre. Stock with a face value of $100 could be exchanged for up to forty acres, costing the average Northern Pacific investor roughly thirty-five cents an acre. Daniel Dodge traveled to Fargo, selected fifteen hundred acres in the Red River valley for which to exchange his railroad stock, and on his return stopped in Kingston to visit. Mary Cowdrey reported that the stock and land prices made the land available to him at the low price of fifteen cents an acre.[27]

The railroad embarked on a campaign to attract settlers and to sell its land, setting up land and immigration departments, sending representatives to recruit European emigrants, and distributing pamphlets throughout Europe and the eastern United States. It sold railroad land for 10 percent down and provided free transportation to those who bought it. The depression of 1873 retarded settlement, but in 1878 the great Dakota boom took off. Between 1878 and 1890 North Dakota's population grew from an estimated 16,000 to 191,000. Cass County, where the Woodwards lived, more than doubled from 8,998 inhabitants in 1880 to 19,613 in 1890.[28]

Industrialization and urbanization created new markets for commercial agriculture, the technology for large-scale cultivation and food processing, and railroads to transport crops to market. New milling processes increased the profitability of the hard spring wheat that thrived in North Dakota and made Minneapolis the flour-milling capital of the country. The price of spring wheat did not rise so fast as the price of spring wheat flour did, a fact that Mary Dodge Woodward frequently lamented. But the high profits from flour stimulated production, which rose from some 843,000 barrels in 1875 to more than 5 million barrels a decade later.[29]

Railroad construction, which resumed in 1877, made the Red River valley the chief supplier of the Minnesota mills. In 1878 James J. Hill organized the purchase of the St. Paul and Pacific Railroad and connected it with the Canadian Pacific to complete a line from St. Paul to Winnipeg. The following year he and some associates absorbed it into a new railroad, the St. Paul, Minneapolis, and Manitoba (called the Manitoba), and began to supply North Dakota and the Red River valley with rails. By 1884 Hill had built two east-west lines and two north-south lines in northern Dakota Territory.[30]

At the 1878 inception of the boom, there was only the main Northern Pacific line from Fargo to Bismarck. Ten years later the Manitoba had 998 miles of track in North Dakota, the reorganized Northern Pacific, 814. In 1884 the Northern Pacific carried 5.7 million bushels of wheat to the Minnesota mills, the Manitoba, 20.7 million. North Dakota had 2.7 million acres planted in wheat in 1890.[31] Cass County wheat had an easy route to market through the railhead at Fargo.

The railroads encouraged agricultural development in order to fill their grain cars. The result was "bonanza farms," huge enterprises run for profit, dedicated to the production of "No. 1 hard" spring wheat and closer to modern agribusiness than to the family homestead more commonly pictured on the nineteenth-century frontier. George W. Cass, president of the Northern Pacific, and Benjamin Cheney, a director of the company, pioneered bonanza farming in the Red River valley. They bought some thirteen thousand acres of Northern Pacific land near Castleton and hired Oliver Dalrymple, a Yale Law School graduate who had owned a large wheat farm near St. Paul, to manage it. The Cass-Cheney investment stimulated the sale of 2.9 million acres of Northern Pacific land by 1880, most of it within a hundred miles of the Red River. The largest purchasers were the Grandin brothers, Pennsylvania bankers who eventually bought sixty-three thousand acres, forty thousand of which Dalrymple managed. Speculators started hundreds of bonanza farms, ranging upward in size from one thousand acres.[32]

The scale of operations on these farms was enormous. In 1879 Dalrymple used 400 horses and mules, 100 seeders, 50 harrows, and 115 harvesters and hired 400 workers at the peak of the harvest season. By 1880 he was supervising 55,000 acres, but not quite half of it was being farmed.[33] Mary Dodge Woodward called Dalrymple the "bonanza farm king" of the region. "His crop has been known to exceed 600,000 bushels," she wrote, "and as many as 195 reapers are used. . . . That ought to give eastern people an idea of the scale on which farming is conducted in Dakota Territory."[34]

Daniel Dodge's operation was small by comparison. Following the harvest of his first crop in 1882, he decided that his farm was not being well managed and asked Walter Woodward to take over. Thereafter he was an absentee owner who visited each summer to oversee the harvest. If Dodge's was a speculative venture, he chose his land wisely. By 1883 land prices in Cass County were ranging between fifteen and twenty-five dollars an acre, a considerable mark-up from the purchase price. And his farm was near the growing rail center of Fargo.[35]

In 1890 Fargo was the largest town in North Dakota,

with 5,664 residents, three daily newspapers, five banks, flour mills, and the electric lights Mary Woodward could see from the Dodge farm some eight miles away. It had a theater, which Kate, Fred, and Walter Woodward attended, semiprofessional baseball teams, and extensive Fourth of July celebrations that included speeches, races, and other sports.[36]

The bonanza farms caught the public imagination, and popular and farm publications spread the story of the grain empire. Laborers flocked to the area for the short, intense growing season. Some worked in the lumber camps of Minnesota and Wisconsin during the winter. Some were college students saving for another year of school. Many were Norwegian and German immigrants trying to raise cash to last them until their own farms were producing. On the Dodge farm many of the hands were Irish immigrants. They earned from $1.75 to $2.50 a day and board. Mary Woodward fretted that they would lose their money to the liquor she despised. Many a spree absorbed a summer's wages.[37]

Daniel Dodge's interests in railroads, land, and wheat brought Mary Dodge Woodward to the northern prairies. They also differentiated her experiences from those of many other western women. However important bonanza farms were to the development of commercial agriculture, they were not the average North Dakota farm household. By 1890 only 1.4 percent of all farms in North Dakota were one thousand acres or larger.[38]

Mary Woodward was, in many ways, atypical. The majority of Dakotans were neither female, the children of native-born citizens, nor elderly. Of the North Dakota population in 1890, some 44 percent were women, and an equal proportion were foreign born. Most of the native-born majority were second-generation immigrants, and only one resident in five had native-born parents.[39] The immigrants were overwhelmingly Norwegians, Germans from Russia, Canadians, Germans, and Swedes.[40] Cass County was similar—45.8 percent female and 39.5 percent foreign born. Only 9 percent of all North Dakotans and 12 percent of Cass County residents were, like Mary Dodge Woodward, native-born females with native-born parents.[41] Woodward was typical in only two respects—she was Caucasian, and, like most native-born adults, she had been born in another state. Wisconsin ranked second only to Minnesota as their predominant birthplace, reflecting a common pattern of movement to nearby frontiers.[42]

Mary Woodward's children, however, were more typical of the native born than was she. Most North Dakotans were young. Almost a third of the population was between the ages of five and twenty, and half of all females were younger than twenty.[43] Given such extreme youth, few settlers shared Woodward's experience, including the grief and uncertainty of widowhood. Only 3.5 percent of all females and 2 percent of all males were widowed. These figures included children; a somewhat higher proportion of adults had probably lost a spouse.[44] Older women, not surprisingly, were more likely to be widowed: 36.6 percent of all women over fifty-five had experienced their husband's death. But there were few older women. Only 3.3 percent of all females in 1890 were between the ages of fifty-five and sixty-four (Woodward was sixty-four when she died that year); only 5.6 percent were fifty-five or older.[45] Few of Woodward's neighbors were truly her contemporaries.

The Woodward family was slightly smaller than the North Dakota average of 4.75 persons per family in 1890, or Cass County's 5.28. But the scope of bonanza farm operations meant that the "household" was larger than the average 4.82 persons per dwelling for the state, or the 5.37 county average.[46] Of all households in the state in 1890 only 2 percent held more than ten people.[47] On the Dodge farm, a few hired workers, like John Martin, the "man-of-all-work," lived year-round with the family. A few returned annually, like Dominic Devanny from Kingston, who came each summer to work. During threshing the Woodward "household" could swell to more than thirty. Furthermore, building construction meant carpenters and well diggers were added to the household.[48]

Despite the added work of caring for these crews, the Woodwards were privileged and lived in greater comfort than did other settlers. There were twelve buildings on the spread by 1887, including the house, horse barn, cow barn, two large granaries, machine house, blacksmith shop, pig pen, and ice house. The house included a sitting room, dining room, kitchen, and large storeroom, besides the bedrooms. Whatever Mary Dodge Woodward's personal assets were (or were not), her cousin's wealth and her son's position assured her of a fair degree of comfort, and even luxury. She was well aware of her class position, and she worried during blizzards about the neighbors who could not burn coal day and night as the Woodwards did. If she was often cold, she nonetheless occupied "the warmest room in Dakota."[49]

Woodward frequently reflected the ethnic and racial biases common to those of her class and background. Her attitudes toward immigrants, Blacks, and Indians were ethnocentric and prejudiced. She had little sympathy for the Indians who had been driven off their land. Through the particular filters of her biases, we see nonetheless the ethnic diversity of the West, including Indians, Germans, Mennonites, Norwegians, and Irish.

Mary Dodge Woodward used a spyglass, or telescope,

to view her world, and through her words we are tele-scoped into an important chapter of western development. Her granddaughter called it "a time of adventure, excitement, and romance," and assumed that the novelty of the experience inspired her grandmother's diary.[50] But the bottom line on the Dodge farm was profit, not drama or adventure. "There is no romance about this country," Woodward wrote. "It is just plain business, and No. 1 hard at that."[51]

Woodward wrote about what she saw: the epic procession of reapers and threshing crews, the wildflowers and birds, the stupendous mirages that could make the wintry prairie an optical wonderland.[52] Many entries are understandably preoccupied with the weather, which could vary from numbing blizzards to extreme heat, from dust storms to downpours. Temperature, precipitation, and prairie fires affected not just personal comfort and safety but the prospects for each year's crops as well.

Woodward provides a front-row view of Dakota's boom days. Yet she herself did not venture away from the farm after 1884. Beyond its boundaries, she remained an observer. She chose to relate to the outside world through voracious reading and knew more about literature, national politics, and the concerns of distant kin, whose letters she relished, than she did about her neighbors. Her isolation was partly a product of the society of commercial agriculture and the transiency of the frontier. "People come and go; families move in and out, and nobody asks whence they came nor whither they go," Woodward wrote. After living six years in Dakota she did not know who lived in half of the farms she could see from her door step.[53] Woodward's homebound life was partly her choice, whether because there were few gatherings that attracted her, few people her own age with whom to talk, or sheer personal preference, we do not know. She was especially lonely when Kate was gone but did not seek the company of other women. Certainly there were amusements and gatherings that attracted the younger members of the household. But the focus on profit seems to have crowded out community. Except for Kate Woodward's brief tenure as a Sunday school superintendent, we find little of women's "community building" in *The Checkered Years*.

Partly because she was not fully engaged in local society, partly because she did not write for an audience, and partly because her diaries were edited for publication, the pictures Woodward provides are often like isolated patchwork squares. A reader must work imaginatively to piece them together, to see a pattern that is larger than the particularity of Woodward's experience.

Woodward focused on the internal and the domestic, and her portrait of the household's seasonal patterns is a valuable historical contribution. The seasons and the accompanying agricultural calendar shaped the annual cycle of activities for everyone. They shaped the household as well. During the slack times from threshing to spring seeding, the family could be as small as Mary Woodward and one or two of her children, as the others left to visit friends and family. Kate was gone during the winter of 1883–84; Fred left for Wisconsin in September 1884 and remained away until spring. Fred had scarcely arrived when Nellie went to visit her mother in Dakota. In February 1885 Walter spent several weeks in Wisconsin, returning with Fred in early March. Again, Fred was gone from December 1885 until March 1886, and Kate was away from January until May. She brought Nellie back with her for a month along with Theron Woodward's two children, Hattie and Mortie. During the winter of

1886–87, all the Woodwards stayed on the farm, but the next fall Fred left again and was gone until February 1888. As soon as he returned, Walter left for more than a month. Kate went to Wisconsin in the fall of 1888 to visit Nellie and the children, and, her mother hoped, to improve her health. Other visitors and the farm workforce periodically swelled this shifting family group. A neighbor, Harry Green, visited frequently to court Kate. And Daniel Dodge came every summer.

Work followed the seasons. From planting through threshing, all hands were needed. As soon as winter broke, in late March or April, the men began seeding. "The boys have been hauling machinery and wheat," Woodward recorded on April 3, 1884, "and now business will begin in earnest and will not cease until the wheat is gathered in." A few weeks later she wrote, "The country is alive with teams." Men and horses walked some twenty miles a day during the arduous spring seeding that, given the short growing season, must be done as quickly as possible. "They rush things here," Woodward wrote.[54]

After seeding came plowing new land, backsetting (turning back the rows in newly plowed land), and weeding. In July there was haying, and in August, the harvest. A phalanx of twine binders – eight on the Dodge farm in 1884 – moved across the fields, often with managers, a mechanic with spare parts, and a wagon carrying twine and water. Mary Woodward's August entries recorded Walter's trips to Fargo for the huge quantities of binding twine the enterprise required. After the harvest came threshing, with enormous work crews, teams of horses, separators, and steam engines moving through the fields. Many of the workers left after threshing. Those who remained began plowing, turning the stubble, and backsetting.

Mary Woodward's daily routine resembled that of many farm women, but with important differences related to class and scale. She brought in some cash with her butter and eggs, and the Woodwards raised vegetables, chickens, and pigs.[55] But the primary focus was wheat. Much food was purchased, a small expense compared to the investment in livestock and machinery necessary to work the land. During the crucial wheat-growing season the women sustained the enormous work crews, and part of their responsibility was preserving and managing food supplies to last through the heavy harvest demand. While the men fixed machinery, ground blades, and oiled reapers, the women cooked and preserved to exhaustion to feed the agricultural workforce. By 1888 three cows on the Dodge farm were producing milk, and Mary Woodward made fourteen pounds of butter a week, not for sale, but to pack away for the harvest crews.[56]

During the 1884 haying the women sent dinner to the fields daily for thirteen men. "I have to rack my brains every day to contrive meals for them," Woodward wrote. Harvest and threshing were the busiest times for the women as well as the men. On one day during the 1885 harvest Woodward reported that she baked seventeen loaves of bread, "making seventy-four loaves since last Sunday, not to mention twenty-one pies, and puddings, cakes, and doughnuts."[57] Threshing brought the heaviest domestic burdens of all. Serving supper to the whole crew could take two or three hours, excluding the preparation time. Frequently during the harvest season the work got so heavy that women – often recent immigrants who spoke little English – were hired to help in the kitchen. Some were married, working to raise cash for family homesteads. The four dollars a week they earned was considerably less than any man's wages but enough to attract a succession of women to the Woodward's kitchen, since domestic work was one of the few occupations considered respectable for a married woman.

Mary Woodward barely tolerated most of them, but she and Kate simply could not handle the work alone. During the 1887 harvest there were fifteen teams at work and thirty mouths to feed besides the family. The burden was too much. That year and again in 1888, a male cook fed sixteen men from a cookstove in the blacksmith shop, while the women took care of the other half of the "household."

The heaviest labor was done by September, the fall plowing by October. Then the winter lull began. "There is nothing much for men to do in Dakota in winter," Woodward wrote. The men hunted, hauled wood, and did other work that was impossible during the growing season. But their daily chores consisted mostly of caring for livestock and supplying fuel and water for the house. For women the domestic chores continued year-round, lighter because the household was smaller, but arduous nonetheless, given the weather, household technology, and the winter exodus of domestic help along with the temporary farm laborers. For Mary Woodward the slack period meant she could sleep in until six A.M. rather than rising at five or earlier.

Valuable as is Woodward's portrait of women's work, she and her female contemporaries were much more than their labor. In isolation or out of context, Woodward's words could reduce her to a "civilizer" or a "drudge." She was neither. Mary Dodge Woodward left her "old brown house" in Kingston reluctantly. She missed her husband and longed for Nellie, Theron, and other family members in Wisconsin. She was disturbed because the Sabbath was not kept as a day of rest, wanted to ban alcoholic beverages, read voraciously, and appreciated culture. But she was not a "reluctant pioneer" pining for the civilized East. She worked extremely hard and was dependent on male kin for her support. But she was more than a helpmate and far from oppressed.

Woodward's deceptively simple chronicle reveals a complex woman. It contradicts stereotypes of western women and reveals much about gender roles, about aging, and about the West itself. Woodward, like most women of her race, class, and time, believed that men and women properly inhabited separate spheres and performed complementary functions. Women provided for the domestic needs of their households. Not until illness confined her to bed at age fifty-seven did Mary Woodward's sons ever get their own breakfast.[58] She nonetheless described adaptations and flexibility in men's and women's roles, recording matter-of-factly that Katie briefly drove a harvester, that Walter helped her with the laundry and churning, and frequently mentioning the neighboring Lessing sisters who plowed, planted, harvested, hauled, and shoveled snow "like men." Woodward felt sorry for the Lessings, not because they did hard work (she recognized that domestic labor was hard), but because they did domestic work as well as their more "masculine" tasks and because she thought their father cruel and controlling. We do not know from *The Checkered Years* how the sisters themselves felt about their lot, whether they embraced the outdoor work or felt burdened by it. Whatever her own feelings, Woodward reveals numerous instances of women and men adapting older roles to new circumstances and the new environment.

Woodward herself found it harder to adapt to the prospect of being dependent and being unneeded. She attempted, during her Dakota years, to reconcile her understanding of herself as domestic partner with her new reality of widowhood and dependent old age. Family was crucial to her, and her greatest fear was that she would lose it. It was as if by planting herself firmly on the farm she made a statement about her own domestic core.

She considered Dakota hers as much as any other settler's and combined her love for its beauties with a practical appreciation of its commercial value. When someone called it "a God-forsaken country," she tartly replied that "the whole of Cass County was covered with No. 1 hard wheat, and the wayside was all abloom with goldenrod and asters which proves that God has not forsaken it."[59]

Despite her sense of belonging, she was, in one important regard, typical – she left. It was not an easy leavetaking. She wrote that never again did she "expect to be considered nor consulted as to where I should rather live." Nonetheless she added, "I'll keep up with the procession as long as I am able." She refused to imitate her sister Isabinda, of whom she wrote, "her heart is in her husband's grave," and who refused "to get any enjoyment out of life without him."[60]

When Daniel Dodge contemplated selling, she said that leaving the farm would "seem like again leaving home." Home for her, finally, was less place than kin and feeling useful. Kingston, she said, was the only place she could "think of as home." But, she added, "when I do get there it will not be home to me without my children." She dreaded leaving the farm because it meant breaking up the family that provided the central meaning in her life. She did not want to lose everyone "who needs or wants me."[61]

The family dispersed after they left the Dodge farm. Walter married Carrie M. Howard, a graduate of Mt. Carroll Seminary and principal of the Oconomowoc, Wisconsin, high school. They moved to Two Harbors, Minnesota, where she served periodically as county school superintendent, and he, as postmaster, justice of the peace, and recorder. They had two children, Ruth Elinor in 1891 and John Paul in 1894. Fred moved with them to Two Harbors to help with business. His mother's frequently expressed concerns about his health proved accurate, and he died on April 8, 1892.[62] Kate went with her mother to Kingston where they gardened and sewed during the short time left. Mary Dodge Woodward died in Kingston on December 25, 1890. All of her children were with her.

Six months later, on June 24, 1891, Kate Woodward married Harry Green, the persistent suitor of her mother's diary, and returned to North Dakota, the only Woodward who settled there permanently. Her years on the Dodge farm were good preparation. The Greens owned three thousand acres at Leal, Barnes County.[63]

Less than three months after Mary Dodge Woodward died, her namesake arrived. Mary Woodward Boynton, Nellie's only child, was born on March 7, 1891.[64] She never met the grandmother whose diaries she published. If they were for her a personal legacy, *The Checkered Years* makes them ours as well.

As a window to our common past, the greatest value of Mary Dodge Woodward's writing is not just that it revises older images of womanhood and the West, but that she reminds us that all images are partial. If she contradicted stereotypes of western women, Woodward did not replace them with anything more "typical." Instead, she helps us to recognize their diversity.

*Elizabeth Jameson*

xxxii

# NOTES

I want to thank Laura Haas of Kingston, Wisconsin, for allowing me to read her correspondence with Ruth Woodward Collins, and Sarah Rubinstein for her help and encouragement. I am particularly grateful to Jane Reilly for outstanding assistance in trying to locate records of the Woodward family in Wisconsin.

1. The stereotypes of western women are defined in Beverly Stoeltje, "A Helpmate for Man Indeed: The Image of the Frontier Woman," *Journal of American Folklore* 88 (January-March 1975): 27–31. For more accurate accounts of the lives of "bad women" in the West, see Marion S. Goldman, *Gold Diggers and Silver Miners: Prostitution and Social Life on the Comstock Lode* (Ann Arbor: University of Michigan Press, 1981); Anne M. Butler, *Daughters of Joy, Sisters of Misery: Prostitutes in the American West, 1865–90* (Urbana: University of Illinois Press, 1985); and Mary Murphy, "The Private Lives of Public Women: Prostitution in Butte, Montana, 1878–1917," *Frontiers* 7 (1984): 30–35, also in Susan Armitage and Elizabeth Jameson, eds., *The Women's West* (Norman: University of Oklahoma Press, 1987), 193–206.

2. For accounts of women settlers, see Lillian Schlissel, Vicki L. Ruiz, and Janice Monk, eds., *Western Women: Their Land, Their Lives* (Albuquerque: University of New Mexico Press, 1988); Armitage and Jameson, eds., *Women's West;* Glenda Riley, *Frontierswomen: The Iowa Experience* (Ames: Iowa State University Press, 1981); Sheryll Patterson-Black, "Women Homesteaders on the Great Plains Frontier," *Frontiers* (Spring 1976): 67–88; John Mack Faragher, *Women and Men on the Overland Trail* (New Haven: Yale University Press, 1979); Julie Roy Jeffrey, *Frontier Women: The Trans-Mississippi West, 1840–1880* (New York: Hill and Wang, 1979); Sandra L. Myres, *Westering Women and the Frontier Experience, 1800–1915* (Albuquerque: University of New Mexico Press, 1982); and Linda Rasmussen, Lorna Rasmussen, Candace Savage, and Anne Wheeler, eds. *A Harvest Yet to Reap: A History of Prairie Women* (Toronto: Women's Press, 1976).

3. For women's work roles, see Joan M. Jensen, *With These Hands: Women Working on the Land* (Old Westbury, N.Y.: Feminist Press, 1981); Patterson-Black, "Women Homesteaders"; Corlann Gee Bush, "The Barn Is His, The House Is Mine: Agricultural Technology and Sex Roles," in *Energy and Transport: Historical Perspectives on Policy Issues,* ed. George H. Daniels and Mark H. Rose (Berkeley: Sage, 1982),

235-59; Laurie K. Mercier, "Women's Economic Role in Montana Agriculture: 'You Had to Make Every Minute Count'," *Montana: The Magazine of Western History* 38 (Autumn 1988): 50-61; Joan M. Jensen, " 'I've Worked, I'm Not Afraid of Work': Farm Women in New Mexico, 1920-1940," in *New Mexico Women: Intercultural Perspectives*, ed. Joan M. Jensen and Darlis A. Miller (Albuquerque: University of New Mexico Press, 1986); Deborah Fink, " 'Mom, It's a Losing Proposition': The Decline of Women's Subsistence Production on Iowa Farms," *North Dakota Quarterly* 52 (Winter 1984): 26-33; Glenda Riley, " 'Not Gainfully Employed': Women on the Iowa Frontier, 1833-1870," *Pacific Historical Review* 49 (May 1980): 237-64; Katherine Harris, "Sex Roles and Work Patterns among Homesteading Families in Northwestern Colorado, 1873-1920," *Frontiers* 7 (1984): 43-49, and in Armitage and Jameson, eds., *Women's West*, 165-78; Kathleen Underwood, "The Pace of Their Own Lives: Teacher Training and the Life Course of Western Women," *Pacific Historical Review* 55 (November 1986): 513-30; and Polly Welts Kaufman, *Women Teachers on the Frontier* (New Haven: Yale University Press, 1984). Recent studies of woman suffrage in the West include Carolyn Stefanco, "Networking on the Frontier: The Colorado Women's Suffrage Movement, 1876-1893," in Armitage and Jameson, eds., *Women's West*, 265-76; Paula Petrik, *No Step Backward: Women and Family on the Rocky Mountain Mining Frontier, Helena, Montana, 1865-1900* (Helena: Montana Historical Society Press, 1987), chapter 6; and Virginia Scharff, "The Case for Domestic Feminism: Woman Suffrage in Wyoming," *Annals of Wyoming* 56 (Fall 1984): 29-37. See also Elizabeth Jameson, "Women as Workers, Women as Civilizers: True Womanhood in the American West," *Frontiers* 7 (1984): 1-8; also in Armitage and Jameson, eds., *Women's West*, 145-64.

4. Patterson-Black, "Women Homesteaders." See also Glenda Riley, "Introduction," Edith Eudora Kohl, *Land of the Burnt Thigh* (New York: Funk and Wagnalls, Inc., 1938; St. Paul: Minnesota Historical Society Press, Borealis Books, 1986), ix-xxxii. For first-hand accounts see Kohl, and Elinor Pruitt Stewart, *Letters of a Woman Homesteader* (Lincoln: University of Nebraska Press, 1961).

5. Mary Dodge Woodward, *The Checkered Years* (Caldwell, Idaho: Caxton Printers, Ltd., 1937; St. Paul: Minnesota Historical Society Press, Borealis Books, 1989), 26, 154, 124.

6. *Checkered Years*, 186, 260, 250.

7. Percy Emmons Woodward, comp., *Some Descendants of Nathaniel Woodward, Mathematician* (Newtonville, Mass.: Rumford Press, 1940), 51; [Mary Boynton Cowdrey], "Introduction," in *Checkered Years*, 8.

8. Theron Royal Woodward, *Dodge Genealogy: Descendants of Tristram Dodge* (Chicago: Lanward Pub. Co., 1904), 71.

9. [Cowdrey], in *Checkered Years*, 8; Theron Woodward, *Dodge Genealogy*, 71.

10. Wisconsin was apparently not the Beaches' first move. Their first two children were born in Canada, the third in Hinesburg in 1849. The fourth child, John Theron, was born in Oasis, Wisconsin, November 14, 1851, as was a fifth in 1854. The last three children were born in Plainfield in 1856, 1858, and 1860. Theron Woodward, *Dodge Genealogy*, 70–71.

11. Theron Woodward, *Dodge Genealogy*, 70–72.

12. Theron Woodward, *Dodge Genealogy*, 71.

13. Theron Woodward, *Dodge Genealogy*, 71. See also *Directory 1869: County Histories of the "Old Northwest"*, Series 1: Wisconsin; Samuel Ower, Government Plats, Green Lake County Abstracts, 1857; Map, Green Lake County, Wisconsin, 1860; Map, Green Lake County, 1875 – all in the Area Resource Center, Forrest R. Polk Library, University of Wisconsin-Oshkosh.

14. Theron Woodward, *Dodge Genealogy*, 71.

15. *Checkered Years*, 148–49, 56, 104.

16. On September 26, 1894, Theron Woodward married Estelle Clark King, a widow sixteen years younger than he. They had three children, two of whom survived infancy: Najah Estelle Woodward, born October 16, 1895, Emory Clark Woodward, born February 27, 1900, and Theron Royal Woodward, who lived less than a year, from July 29, 1897, to June 8, 1898. Theron Woodward, *Dodge Genealogy*, 71, 73–74.

17. Theron Woodward, *Dodge Genealogy*, 75; [Cowdrey], in *Checkered Years*, 8–9; *Checkered Years*, 52–53.

18. John D. Hicks, *The Populist Revolt: A History of the Farmers' Alliance and the People's Party* (Minneapolis: University of Minnesota Press, 1931; Lincoln: University of Nebraska Press, 1961), 3–4. Accounts vary slightly regarding exactly how much land the railroads received. John A. Garraty, *The New Commonwealth, 1877–1890* (New York: Harper & Row, New American Nations Series, 1968), 9, gives the figure as 128 million acres for the period 1862–71.

19. Elwyn B. Robinson, *History of North Dakota* (Lincoln: University of Nebraska Press, 1966), 54–67.

20. See *Checkered Years*, 76. The bias in Cowdrey's footnoted explanation is apparent.

21. Robinson, *History of North Dakota*, 118–19, 110.

22. Robinson, *History of North Dakota*, 122–27; Melvin E. Kazeck, *North Dakota: A Human and Economic Geography* (Fargo: North Dakota Institute for Regional Studies, North Dakota Agricultural College, 1956), 25, 176–78.

23. Garraty, *New Commonwealth*, 9.

24. Robinson, *History of North Dakota*, 148–50.

25. Robinson, *History of North Dakota*, 125–26.

26. Robinson, *History of North Dakota*, 126–27.

27. Kazeck, *North Dakota*, 25; [Cowdrey], in *Checkered Years*, 8, 10. Kazeck figured the average price of land at 37 cents an acre. A purchaser who received forty acres for $14 would spend 35 cents per acre.

28. Robinson, *History of North Dakota*, 131–32, 134; United States, *Census*, 1890, *Population*, part 1, p. 307.

29. Robinson, *History of North Dakota*, 133–36.

30. Robinson, *History of North Dakota*, 140–42.

31. Robinson, *History of North Dakota*, 142, 143, 135–36; U.S., *Census*, 1890, *Population*, part 3, p. 636–37.

32. Robinson, *History of North Dakota*, 137, says that the land totaled 13,440 acres and that Dalrymple first sowed it in spring 1876; Kazeck, *North Dakota*, 26, says that the farm was 12,000 acres and was first planted in 1875. See Robinson, 137–39, and Kazeck, 26–27. For a study of bonanza farming, see Hiram M. Drache, *The Day of the Bonanza: A History of Bonanza Farming in the Red River Valley of the North* (Fargo: North Dakota Institute for Regional Studies, 1964).

33. Robinson, *History of North Dakota*, 138. Kazeck, *North Dakota*, 27, says that Dalrymple supervised the cultivation of 34,000 acres of grain in 1885. He delegated responsibility to three superintendents, each responsible for 8,000 acres; foremen directly supervised 2,000 acres each, thus approximating Walter Woodward's managerial responsibility.

34. *Checkered Years*, 129.

35. Robinson, *History of North Dakota*, 150.

36. Robinson, *History of North Dakota*, 155, 165.

37. Kazeck, *North Dakota*, 27; Robinson, *History of North Dakota*, 138–39; *Checkered Years*, 228, 94, 138, 237.

38. U.S., *Census*, 1890, *Population*, part 3, p. 610.

39. U.S., *Census*, 1890, *Population*, part 1, p. 468–69, part 3, p. 234.

40. Kazeck, *North Dakota*, 35.

41. U.S., *Census*, 1890, *Population*, part 1, p. 634–35.

42. Robinson, *History of North Dakota*, 146. Although North Dakota was less than 1 percent Black, it should be noted that the 1890 census enumerated only Blacks and Whites and omitted American Indians, thus misrepresenting the racial and ethnic composition of the state. See U.S., *Census*, 1890, *Population*, part 1, p. 468–69, part 3, p. 14–17.

43. U.S., *Census*, 1890, *Population*, part 1, p. 747; 27.3 percent of the population was between the ages of five and seventeen; 5.2 percent was between eighteen and twenty. The proportion of the female population under age twenty was computed from U.S., *Census*, 1890, *Population*, part 3, p. 234.

44. Fifty-eight percent of all females and 66.6 percent of all males were

single, reflecting the youth of the total population. Still, almost 40 percent of all females were married, a figure that accounted for most adult women. Compiled from U.S., *Census*, 1890, *Population*, part 3, p. 125.

45. Compiled from U.S., *Census*, 1890, *Population*, part 3, p. 162. Some persons who lost spouses may have remarried, and remarriage may account for the lower proportion of men who were listed as widowed.

46. U.S., *Census*, 1890, *Population*, part 1, p. 870.

47. U.S., *Census*, 1890, *Population*, part 1, p. 898–99. The exact size of "households" would depend on when during the annual work cycle the census taker arrived and whether temporary workers were enumerated. Unfortunately the original 1890 manuscript census burned, so it is impossible to check the composition of particular farm households.

48. *Checkered Years*, 144.

49. *Checkered Years*, 201, 208.

50. *Checkered Years*, 208.

51. [Cowdrey], in *Checkered Years*, 9, 11; *Checkered Years*, 208.

52. The mirages that Woodward saw were caused by the bending of light rays in layers of air of varying density. The differences in density were caused by rapid changes in temperature among the layers of atmosphere. For instance, when a cool dense layer of air underlies a heated layer, light rays may reach the eye that were originally directed above the line of sight. The warm air bends light rays, so that an object ordinarily out of view below the horizon will apparently be lifted into the sky. This phenomenon is called looming and accounts for Woodward's ability to see towns and objects many miles distant from the Dodge farm. See *The World Book Encyclopedia*, 1986 ed., s.v. "mirage"; *Encyclopaedia Britannica*, 15th ed., s.v. "mirage."

53. *Checkered Years*, 242.

54. *Checkered Years*, 34, 35–36.

55. Woodward reported one February that she produced seven pounds of butter a week, which would sell for 35 cents a pound in Fargo; *Checkered Years*, 216.

56. *Checkered Years*, 238.

57. *Checkered Years*, 42, 90.

58. *Checkered Years*, 27.

59. *Checkered Years*, 91–92.

60. *Checkered Years*, 213, 174

61. *Checkered Years*, 213, 251–52, 236.

62. Theron Woodward, *Dodge Genealogy*, 74–75, 71.

63. Theron Woodward, *Dodge Genealogy*, 71; C. A. Lounsberry, *North Dakota: History and People, Outlines of American History*, vol. 3 (Chicago: S. J. Clarke Pub. Co., 1917), 895–96.

64. Theron Woodward, *Dodge Genealogy*, 71.

# The Checkered Years

ONE of my earliest recollections is of hearing my mother say, "Someday you will read the diary of your grandmother, who died before you were born." It is the fulfillment of that prophecy which has resulted in this book.

In 1882 there lived in Kingston, a small inland Wisconsin village, Mary Dodge Woodward, then fifty-six years of age. Twenty-five years before, she had come to Wisconsin from Vermont with her husband, John, and her father, known to the family as Gramp, both now dead. Slight, wiry, and fine-featured, with a courage and tenacity of purpose quite out of proportion to her small frame, she was an example of that New England type found frequently in the West in those early years.

The family consisted of five children, now grown: Theron and Nellie, the two eldest, married and gone from the nest many years; Walter, thirty, slender, tall, and capable; Katie, small, dainty, and twenty-three; and Fred, just turned eighteen and hardly away from the playfulness of youth.

They had sprung from a fine old American family. Mary's paternal grandfather, Reverend Jordan Dodge, was a celebrated itinerant

11

Baptist minister of his time, whose wife Lucy was of the President Adams line and a descendant of Stephen Hopkins of the *Mayflower*. Mary's father was an ironmaker, shrewd and intelligent, but unfortunate and improvident as had been his father before him. When little Mary Dodge had been left motherless at the age of nine, she, along with her four small sisters, had been "parceled out" to relatives. It had fallen to her lot to make her home with her great-uncle, John Dodge, a cousin of Governor Henry Dodge, Wisconsin's first Territorial governor.

John Dodge had a son, Daniel, who was by inheritance an ironmaker and inventor and who, in his later years, patented the first machine to manufacture horseshoe nails and thereby acquired wealth. At the time of the failure of the Northern Pacific Railroad in the late seventies, Daniel Dodge, then a resident of Keeseville, New York, held railroad stock which could be turned into land at par and which, at the market price of the stock, would make the land available to him at fifteen cents per acre.

He went to Fargo, Dakota Territory, to select such pieces of land as he desired, and stopped en route at the Woodward home in Wisconsin. Again in 1882, Daniel Dodge went to the Territory to look after the harvesting of his first crop. Finding that the farm was being unsuccessfully managed, he decided to offer Walter Woodward the management at a cash salary of $1,000 and expenses per year, Walter to be the authorized agent for Mr. Dodge in all the latter's transactions in the Territory. Walter accepted and, in the fall of that year, moved with his mother, Fred, and Katie to Dakota.

The Territory was at the height of its boom days. It was a time of adventure, excitement, and romance. In 1883, according to the report of the land commissioner in Washington, eight million acres of government land had been disposed of to private persons within the year. As no person could take more than 320 acres (a pre-emption homestead and a timber claim), this meant that no less than 25,000 and probably more than 35,000 farmers located that year upon government lands alone, without taking into consideration the thousands of acres sold from the railroad land grants. In the spring of 1883, it is said that immigration reached 5,000 in one day; and by the end of the year, 2,161 homesteads had been entered in the Territory. The facetious press of the times reported passenger trains crowded with "comers" and "lookers," hotels filled with cots in halls and parlors until it reminded one of "after the battle, mother";

and firmly averred that no country appeared as frequently in story and print as Dakota.

The Dodge farm, consisting of over two sections (about 1,500 acres), was situated in the very heart of the bonanza farm district of the Red River Valley, known today as "the bread-basket of the world." Proud, indeed, were these early settlers of their vast holdings; their buildings, many of which were fine for those times; their extensive machinery; their live-stock; and their great wheat fields, presenting as they did such a striking contrast to the wild country which had been inhabited only by the warlike Sioux up to the time of the admission of the Territory, a mere twenty years before. Owners and managers came from far and near to assume operation of the farms. Names like Dalrymple, Grandin, Dunlap, Chaffee, and Kindred were famous not only throughout the Territory, but over a large portion of the United States as well.

The chief product of these big farms was, of course, hard wheat, called No. 1 hard, to the raising of which the farmers gave their almost exclusive attention. In 1884 the Northern Pacific Elevator Company handled an average of 75,000 bushels of wheat each day during harvest. One bonanza farmer alone had, at one time, 600,000 bushels of No. 1 hard in the elevators which he was holding for

14

better prices. We may suppose that it was the novelty of these surroundings, the newness of the country, and the uniqueness of her experiences that inspired Mary Dodge Woodward to record her impressions painstakingly, but in a lively manner, day after day, for all the years she spent in Dakota.

There are in existence five volumes of the diary: small, leather-bound books, gilt-edged, and filled with a neat, old-fashioned pen-and-ink handwriting. All of the joys, woes, hopes, fears, humor, optimism, memories of the past, and observations of the present are there set down as a record of her days, in her habit, just as she lived them fifty years ago.

Any suspicion that these writings would ever get into print never entered her mind. On May 1, 1885, she wrote, "I've nobody to talk to except this diary, and here I can say what I please for nobody but my children could ever read it." September 27, 1885, she said, "It is a shame to have this nice book so sketchily and poorly kept, but I am usually tired when I write in it and I haven't taken pains as I ought. I fear the family will fail to make out dates and weather records should they ever wish to." On January 1, 1887, she wrote in rhyme,

"I closed a closely written book last week,
A volume which no eye but mine will seek,
Among the folios laid away.

15

"If on each page I did imprint fair flowers
Of deeds, or naught but leaves of wasted
    hours,
No one save God and I can say."

A large amount of poetry occurs in the five books, over six hundred first lines, mostly in two-, four-, and six-line quotations. Much of it was quoted from memory. The selections were often misquoted or altered to better suit the meaning of the diarist. Explaining her use of it, she wrote December 31, 1886, "The year is about to close, and with it, my ill-kept diary with its blots, mistakes, joys, and sorrows. It seems like taking leave of some old friend. It has offered me much comfort, and helped pass away many leisure moments. I have enjoyed putting down many a pleasant little verse or remembrance which has fitted the day and expressed my thoughts better than I could myself."

Some of the lines are believed to be her own, and these are used just as they occur. Others have been traced to their source by the editor who, to accomplish this purpose, searched through hundreds of poems. Some of the excerpts will forever remain waifs and strays, and these have been used only where their omission would detract from the text. Since a full record was made for every day of the five years, it has been necessary to telescope time to some extent. Only excerpts have been

16

chosen which had to do with some phase of pioneer life on the prairie. No departure from the simple, natural, conversational tone of the language of the original diary has been made.

The editor would like to make grateful acknowledgment to the following firms for their kind permission to use copyrighted material in this book: to Houghton Mifflin Company for the use of quotations from the poems of Longfellow, Whittier, Phoebe Cary, and T. B. Aldrich; to D. Appleton-Century Company for lines from William Cullen Bryant; and to Charles Scribner's Sons for a quotation from Dr. J. G. Holland. Sources consulted by the editor for material used in footnotes were: *Canada Under British Rule*, by John G. Bourinot; *The History of the Northwest Rebellion*, by C. P. Mulvaney; and several histories of North Dakota.

1884

When God made man,
He seemed to think it best
To make him in the East,
And let him travel West.

# 1884

THE NEW YEAR turns from the old reluctantly, as I did from the old brown house, and the wind voices a protest round the gable. The family on the Dodge farm consists, at the present time, of Walter, Fred, and myself. Katie and Theron and Nellie are far away, but we have every reason to believe they are happy, and we feel contented with our lot even though it is a cold one. When I was a child of eight, after my mother died, I was sent to Uncle John's and lived on the Dodge farm in Vermont. Now I am old, my husband is dead, and I am called to live on the Dodge farm in Dakota Territory, just fifty years later.

The temperature is twenty degrees below zero at 8 A. M., which is too cold to work and almost too cold to live. But the sun nearly always shines in Dakota and although the days are cold they are not gloomy. The big coal stove booms night and day and we cannot suffer in the house; however, it is really not safe to be out of doors. Walter froze a spot on his cheek while he and Fred were getting out manure. We are all frostbitten even to Roxy, the dog, and Bjone, the cat.

No mortal hand could paint such beautiful

designs as adorn my kitchen windows, and when the evening sun, descending, sets the sky on fire with redness, they resemble white lamp shades over a bright light. Our neighbors, Mrs. McAuliffe and Rose, have been spending the evening with us. Tonight we saw an *ignis fatuus*, or will-o'-the-wisp.

JANUARY 7

The wind blew this morning, driving the snow before it furiously, but it went down by noon and is now pleasant and warm. Walter and John Martin, who is visiting us, went to Fargo and bought me a pair of slippers which just suit me. If I am to live in Dakota, I find I must prepare for cold. A young McGowan boy froze his feet so badly that they may have to be amputated. Alas, he took just one more drink before going home and wandered about until morning. I think nine-tenths of the people who have frozen to death in Dakota have been under the influence of intoxicating drink. A clear brain is needed to find refuge in a storm.

Nothing can be done out of doors in weather like this except the chores. The boys have had all the care of the nineteen horses this winter. Last year we hired a man who "knew all about horses." Some of them were lousy in the spring. Today a horse ran off and Walter and Fred hooked on a pair and brought him safely in. The boys manage to do a little carpenter work by bringing their tools into the kitchen.

JANUARY 16

Walter and Fred have gone to Fargo. They take advantage of every pleasant hour, there are so few. We get our mail only once a week which seems strange for we have always before lived close to the post office. I was glad indeed to get letters from my two good girls and from my dear sister, Isabinda. There is no road at all between here and Fargo and some of the way the boys could not see one light. No wonder people get lost on the prairie which one of the papers calls a "boundless sea of undulating land," and suggests that everyone should carry a pocket compass and have sense enough to know that the needle always points north. No one should go more than a mile from home without a good, warm coat, for no matter how brightly the sun may be shining, the blizzard season is upon us. The boys brought thirteen newspapers with all the news, good and bad. The burning of *Notre Dame* fills my mind with horror.

We stay in the sitting room near the stove most of the day, going into the kitchen just long enough to eat our meals. Tonight is cold and clear and the stars gleam as I have never seen them except in Dakota. Fred is reading *Foul Play*, and Walter, *Great Expectations*, quite characteristic of the two boys.

JANUARY 19

The sitting room is full of sunshine and I am alone with the exception of Roxy, our dog, and my old rose geranium which really seems a thing of life, it looks so much like home. I tend the plants with the greatest care, fearful lest I may lose them. Besides the geranium, I have only a pot of pansies with never a blossom.

There is no school as diphtheria is among the Mennonites, and there have been several deaths. I hope the epidemic will not reach this neighborhood where there are many children. Mr. McAuliffe got lost last night coming from Fargo, although he has lived here seven years. He wandered around until he finally found a stack with a path leading from it to a house where he remained until morning. I expect my poor cat is dead. I have not seen her these three days.

JANUARY 28

I wanted the boys to go after the mail but they dared not put off the hay. If there should be a blizzard tomorrow, I could get along without mail better than the animals could without eating. The horses look much better than last winter. How they do prance about! Last night was so clear that the stars gleamed and the electric light in Fargo fairly shone into my bedroom window! Who would suppose the town was eight miles away as the crow flies! We can see a good many buildings there with the spyglass since the leaves have fallen.

The wind has blown furiously all day and the snow flies. One can scarcely breathe outdoors. Walter and Fred and I have sat around the fire so many stormy evenings that we do not feel like laughing at the "baffled Fiend as his sounding wing goes by," but, after all, we have plenty to read and plenty to eat, so let it storm! Fred is reading *Pickwick Papers.* Walter is suffering with tooth-ache and, for once, doesn't care for reading. I have been interested in *Judith Shakespeare* and *Nature's Serial Story,* both in *Harper's Magazine.*

FEBRUARY 2

A really nice day and I have washed and dried all the flannels. I have been alone with the exception of Fred who, of all people on earth, is the best one to be with. One cannot be lonesome. Every few minutes a flock of little brown birds alights by the door. They have tippits that look like swan's-down around their necks, which are white. They look lovely to me. Dear little birds, how can they live through the Dakota winters! I have had no eggs this winter and my cakes have been failures. This morning I hunted up Katie's receipts, threw my old brains out of the window, and made a coffee cake.

Walter came home early, before I had begun to look for him—the first time that ever happened. A little later Nora McAuliffe and Johnny came. Fred played them a tune, but the little boy had never heard music before and hid his face in his sister's gown. The McAuliffe's, our nearest neighbors, are a very intelligent family, and we exchange much reading with them. We furnish reading to our German neighbors, the Lessings, who never had any before. I am reading Jane Welsh Carlyle's *Letters*. My diary is a great deal of company for me and I like to write in it. Besides, it lets me do all the talking.

FEBRUARY 8

A bright, pleasant day with no wind. This morning there was a splendid mirage, one of the most beautiful features of this country. The stacks and drifts look like towering monuments of glistening marble. We can see a vast territory rising round us, and trains innumerable which look as though they are sailing through the air. One village or farm will sink from sight while another, farther on, will appear in a moving panorama. The haystacks resemble hourglasses, and the houses appear to be castles stretched three times their usual height. The elevators look like Bartholdi's statue. We can see a dozen from here, also the towns of Durbin, Horace, Mapleton, Davenport, and Casselton. They are mirrored in the clear sky above with no division or space between the real and the reflection.

FEBRUARY 11

Wind blowing, snow flying, cold and blustering and unpleasant and lonesome. I was sick last night and tried in vain to sleep but:

> Outside, the tempest shrieked and roared,
> Inside, old Roxy wheezed and snored;
> It seemed to me a din eternal,
> Kept up from regions of the infernal.

*Nobody will doubt the originality of the above.* The boys had to get their breakfast for the first time in their lives. After the kitchen door was opened, the cold chilled my rose geranium so it drooped. Fred nearly froze pumping water. The Lord help those who have no warm houses in this cold country, how else could they live through the winters! No man could have walked to Green's today and lived.

People say there is more snow out in the

western part of the territory, around the Little Missouri, than there has been for ten years. Many of the Indian tribes are starving, some of them being kept alive on dog and horse flesh. Spotted Elk, the noble red man discharged the other day from the United States district court at Deadwood, said that the weather was too cold to go home and that he preferred to stay in jail at present. Perhaps he was a wise Indian.

### FEBRUARY 20

Sixteen degrees below zero and snowing hard. Walter started early for Fargo and got back at five o'clock bringing plenty of reading: *Harper's Monthly* and the letters. Without material to read we could not live here where the boys are confined to the house every evening. He also brought a little candy so I do not lack all the sweets of life. I hope to see Katie before the Ides of March.

Oh, the dreary winter, how the storm has raged all day! Fred came in with both ears frozen. I guess they will slough off in the spring. The boys try to get a bucket of water apiece to the horses every day.

### MARCH 1

Blustering March comes in like a lion; therefore we may hope that it will be lamblike in its exit. The snow flies so that we cannot see the barn half of the time, and when we do, Fred says there is a mirage. The drifts are mountain high. We can just see the tip of the clothes reel from the east bedroom window. I never saw such a storm in Vermont nor Wisconsin. The boys just asked me if I heard "the merry tootle of its toot—the wild, hilarious music of the tootle of its toot." They sit here playing checkers. No two boys could get along better nor be more companionable than they.

Mr. Green was here yesterday. He says there is no road at all between here and his house, but I suspect if Katie had been here the road would have been better. We have seen his son, Harry, only once this winter.

I suppose Theron is in Wisconsin. How I should like to be at home just as I used to be to meet my boy at the old brown house where we have all met together in the days that are gone, never to return! He has brought his wife Anna's remains from Kansas City so that she may sleep with her mother and other ancestors in the Kingston cemetery. It seems strange to think of her as dead. She was so well and full of life when last I saw her.


MARCH 12

The storm ceased about midnight having raved and raved for forty-eight hours. Nobody can describe a blizzard. There is one kind in which the snow sticks all over everything, and another that is colder, in which the snow drives with terrible force, the sun shining above it. This is the Dakota boomer's exhilarating weather!

We read this account of the experience of three people in a recent blizzard. A young German farmer left his father's house about ten miles from Fargo, in the company of two neighbor boys, for his claim five miles distant. As they were about to return home, the storm burst upon them and they decided to stay in the claim shanty until it was over. They started a fire in an old stove, but their supply of fuel soon ran out and they were forced to burn portions of the building which was protecting them from the storm. Piece by piece the shanty was consumed until, by morning, all that remained of the building was a small portion at one end. Had the storm continued a few hours longer, they would have been without food and shelter.

MARCH 16, SUNDAY

A beautiful day which would be springlike if the snow banks were not so high. Watching for spring here is so very different from that in any other country in which I have ever lived. There are no trees. I cannot look for buds on lilacs or maples. At this time of the year the country is dreary indeed. One sees a vast expanse of snow which is never so heavy, until it becomes mud, that the wind will not take it up and whirl it about. There is no slush here until the winter breaks for good. A flock of snow birds just lit by the door with "quick, glad wings of sunny sheen."

For several nights the sun has been nearly blood-red at sunset. There have been many such sights these past few months. A Prof. Daniel Kirkwood says the phenomenon has been puzzling astronomers. These brilliant glows may be seen about the sun on any clear day in all parts of the habitable world. He thinks the condition is due, either to watery vapor in the atmosphere or meteoric matter from volcanic eruptions in Java and Alaska. All explanations seem to have their difficulties, but we have the sunsets. The comet and the evening star vie with each other in brilliancy. The former is a little above and to the left of the latter. I saw a big white owl.

MARCH 19

A dull morning. The fog flies in the air almost like snow and one might as well be on the boundless ocean for all one can see. I have not seen the electric light in Fargo for the

31

past two nights, which I miss very much for I like to look out in the night and see it gleam as I can from my bedroom window. Nothing but a thick fog or blizzard can shut it off. There has been a fog for six successive mornings, "chilly enough to freeze a dog," as Gramp used to say. We had such weather last spring so there *is* damp weather in Dakota, although one has to live here to find out, for the papers boom the country outrageously.

Katie will be here one week from today, and the week will seem a long one. The boys have had a lonely time here this winter with her away and only an old woman in the house.

MARCH 22

A beautiful, bright morning and the fog has cleared away at last. If I were at home I should be listening for prairie hens and robins but it is too early in the season for that here. Dakotans say we will get another blizzard, but I say not. We have let the coal fire go out for the first time. I have been viewing the country round from the chamber window with the spyglass. I can see from there three larger schoolhouses than I ever saw in Wisconsin: one in Fargo, one in Mapleton, and one in Casselton; besides four country schoolhouses, all painted white. The Dakotan of the next generation should be an educated person.

It has rained a little, snowed a little, and
shone a little as is the way with March. Walter came with Katie and never was I so glad
to see anyone. I have been here all winter
without her, and she was never before away
from home longer than one week. We have
spent what remained of the day talking of
home and friends. How I *did* enjoy it! There
will be no time for reading nor much work
yet awhile. It is raining tonight and lightens
away off to the southwest. I think we may
safely say spring has come to Dakota.

APRIL 1
There are a great many little birds flying
about. They are trim and neat in dark brown
with silver breasts. My little winter friends
with the tippits have gone. Ducks and geese
are extremely plentiful, but they are so wild
that one can seldom get a shot at them, although Fred has his gun in readiness. The
hunters kill the game in great numbers. Two
of our neighbors, in a six-hour hunt, killed
sixty ducks: thirty mallards, and the rest pin-
tails and teals. It seems wrong to take so
many of them. I think they should be protected by law.

The boys got out the wagon and washed the
sleigh ready to stow away. They cut a channel

through the drifts to the tool house to let the water into the sloughs which are rapidly filling up. The water settles back from the Sheyenne River. Walter was up two nights with the horses. They had belly-ache from wading in the cold slough water.

APRIL 3

Walter and Katie went to Fargo in a lumber wagon, he, to get things preparatory to seeding, and she, to take the teacher's examinations. They hired a man named Grimes— maybe a descendant of "that good old man." The boys have been hauling machinery and wheat, and now business will begin in earnest and will not cease until the wheat is gathered in. Walter says if we had fifty two-year-old heifers we might go to Montana and get rich; but Fred can't understand whether he means two-year-olds or yearlings, so we remain poor.

Sitting Bull and One Bull, with an interpreter, passed through Fargo today on their way to St. Paul where they are to make cattle contracts for the Sioux Reservation. They say the old chief looks to be failing. His nose is hooked and is gradually protruding more and more toward his chin. His face is a mass of wrinkles, and in a greasy hunting suit, wolfskin cap and calico shirt, he looks little like the great warrior history will portray.

34

The whole caravan started out this morning at seven o'clock—out onto the good, rich land to seed. What a hubbub they made! Walter is up with the first ray of light, and rings the bell to call up the men so that they can feed their horses and be in to breakfast at six. Farmers are much elated over the early spring.

The country looks God-forsaken now. Everything is mud, and *such* mud, black and heavy and sticky, like glue! I pity the men trudging through it all day on foot. Nobody can imagine what Dakota mud is like until he gets into it and tries to lift his feet. It sticks to the wheels until they are immense; yet the boys made eighteen miles in it today. Fred is a sight one would not see in Wisconsin; covered with mud, even his face. But he comes in dancing and says, "I'd like to call at Gosses." "They'd put you out," Katie replies.

When the sun shines, such a steam arises from the ground that the prairie looks like an ocean with waves. One cannot make out objects at a distance. The country is alive with teams, seeding and dragging. All the seeding must be done at once as there is no hope of securing a good crop unless the seed is in early. Today the boys made nineteen miles each with their seeders. Twenty miles is considered a good day's work with a team of horses. Dakota farmers seem more energetic than the farmers down home. They rush things here. The farms are very large and perhaps men work better in gangs. We have no spare man now, nor horse, nor woman. Katie and I have no time to be lonely. We bake an ovenful of bread daily, eight loaves.

MAY 1

Not a pansy yet. Immense flocks of little gray birds fly over the wheat fields, alighting now and then to pick up wheat. They are welcome to all they can find. A meadow lark just lit on a post in front of the open door and sang to me so sweetly of home. Harry Green called to see Katie. She had the offer of the school, but I could not get a girl and would not give Katie up.

I have been reading *The Queen's Book*. It is written in plain, homespun language and the incidents are graphically described. An "indefatigable Brown" would come in handy on this farm; however, we have John Martin whom we have decided to keep as man-of-all-work on the place this summer. Walter's mechanical ingenuity is very convenient here, where there is so much machinery.

Seventy-six degrees at 2 P. M., and yesterday the men plowed with their overcoats on. The grass begins to grow, and soon the whole prairie will look beautiful indeed. Still, I want to see trees. Perhaps because I was brought up under the Green Mountains in old Vermont. We have fifty acres for a dooryard. All the rest is sowed with grain and now looks like green velvet. Mr. McAuliffe's trees are leafing out, and to look that way almost makes me homesick. He started a tree claim.

I can see fully a hundred farmhouses with the telescope, besides the towns. Who would believe that seven years ago there was not a cabin on the prairie; and five years before that, only three white men lived along the line of the Northern Pacific Railroad between the Red River and Bismarck!

The water has gone out of the sloughs which wind around without end with the appearance of having been a river bed. There was a splendid mirage this morning at five o'clock. As I was going down cellar after butter I stopped and admired it and thought of one whom I should like to have seen it.

Ninety-four this morning and so hot we can scarcely live through the day, yet tonight we will shiver, I know. Walter and Katie had to walk to Fargo. Fred hung the thermometer in the sun and in a few minutes the temperature rose to 104 degrees. There has been thunder and lightning, but not one drop of rain has fallen although the crops need it very much. The sun looks like a great red ball as it nears the horizon. It has no rays, any more than the moon. The air is like an arid desert during the warm weather, for there is no bushing or timber to cool it.

MAY 21

The rain has been coming down slowly and steadily since ten o'clock, just the right sort to bring up the garden seeds. I am thinking how nice my flower garden must be looking at home, with the tulips in bloom. Here, I have only four or five pansy plants in a little bed under the bedroom window, which comprises my Dakota flower garden. There are still plenty of leaves on the old geranium which, with the help of the big coal stove, has braved a Dakota winter.

MAY 23

The rain has poured steadily for forty-eight hours. The cistern is running over, the ground is soaked, and the crops are likely to be drowned. Dakota is a great land for extremes, either too hot or too cold, too wet or too dry. I cannot dig in the dirt here. I tried to cut out a sod in the front yard, but the soil clung to the ax like gum. There are eight pansy blossoms out after the rain. They look like the faces of old, familiar friends, almost human. I never see one without thinking of John. He and I used to love to watch them at home.

This evening, just at dark, the sky looked perfectly frightful. It has been ablaze with lightning ever since until now, eleven o'clock. I called Walter to sit with me, for I am nervous in storms. The lightning seems so much brighter here than at home. We can see so much sky.

JUNE 1

Well diggers are here. One of them has never been east of the Mississippi River, decidedly a western man. We already have two wells on the place, one bored and one dug, but they do not afford half enough water for the horses around harvest-time. One of our neighbors dug sixteen wells, and finally moved to a place about ten miles away where there was water. Our diggers are down over sixty feet. A great variety of stones come out of the well, all smooth and wave-washed. I think this has once been all water. Now there's none. If a well in Dakota does not fill up at once when water is reached, it soon fails.

Every time Fred sees me writing in my diary, he asks me how far I have gotten. He just said, "Have you gotten through August?"

JUNE 15

The roses are beginning to bloom and all Dakota is literally covered with them. The roadways are bordered with roses and scarlet-eyed daisies. Walter picked some strawberries. I am sure they would grow in abundance under cultivation, but nobody tries to grow anything here except No. 1 hard wheat.

Roxy followed the boys into the field where they are pulling mustard. Walter heard her cry and found her nearly dead with the heat. He fetched her in and poured water on her.

There are dozens of tree claims in this vicinity. Some look well; others have been deserted after the owners proved up their homesteads and these, of course, look neglected and straggling. Where the trees have been cultivated there are hedges of wild roses growing between the rows. They look beautiful.

Tom is backsetting. When we first came here we thought that a queer word, but soon, Dakota-like, we caught it.[1] People mentioned

---

[1] The word "backset," as used by the Dakota farmer, means to turn back the rows of earth which have previously been plowed.

The Old Brown House, Home of the Woodwards in Kingston, Wisconsin

Public School, Mapleton, Dakota Territory

Threshing Scene, Dakota Territory

Walter Beach Woodward, Manager of the Dodge Farm

the autumn as the usual time to backset. That was called the "fall backset." Autumn was the time when the Indians usually revolted, and the inhabitants were wont to remark that they wondered if the Indians would give them a "fall backset" that year. With every pioneering step the settler makes a contribution to an appendix to Webster.

JULY 10

Nobody can imagine how beautiful the wheat fields look, whole sections without a break waving in the breeze. What would the old Vermonters say of it? I wish they could see Cass County now, just as it stands, one vast ocean of wheat.

Walter took me over to Shell's today. They live close to the Sheyenne River, and it seems quite homelike there among the trees. The river is a muddy, sluggish stream, and on this level land it winds around, nearly surrounding Shell's house. There are oaks, cottonwoods, boxelders, grape vines, and raspberries growing there. I suppose they would have grown anywhere on the prairies except for the fires which, before any of the sod was broken, must have run with terrible force when once they started. I have seen some great fires since I came here.

Fred brought a Swedish girl named Mary

who cannot speak one word of English. I hate to bother with her, but we must have someone. Walter went to Sampson's this evening for eggs and I went along for the ride. I love to ride over these beautiful prairies when the wind doesn't blow. We found some exquisite daisies, orange-colored leaves with bright scarlet stamens. I wish we could send them to friends at home.

JULY 20

Walter took me to Mapleton this morning. I had never been there. We went past sixteen miles of wheat, going one road and coming home another past our Hayes farm.[1] All was wheat and oats as far as the eye could reach, with a few fields of barley. Almost all the land is broken and is good, rich black grain-growing soil. Mapleton is about the size of Kingston, not so many dwellings but more business blocks.

We had new potatoes today. Dakota is a fine place for vegetables, especially peas. We have great quantities of them. The men are haying, all thirteen of them, and we send their dinners to the fields. I have to rack my brains every day to contrive meals for them.

---

[1] The Hayes farm was one which Mr. Daniel Dodge had bought for his friend, Jerry Hayes, of Keeseville, New York, who had been unable to make the payments, so that Mr. Dodge had to take it over.

Tonight I went out of doors and there, by the corner of the house, stood three tramps. They wanted to sleep in the barn, so Walter took them some blankets. Apparently they did not dare go up to the granary where the boys were. The country is full of men tramping about and begging at farm houses where they stop to hire out. I have fed several the past week and so have my neighbors. Fortunately we are too far from the tracks to be bothered with regular tramps, but they go by the elevators in droves.

JULY 31

Walter said he must go to town for supplies and I decided to go with him. I wanted to buy some pillows for the granary and some odd pieces of crockery which I wished to select myself. We took dinner at the Continental. I enjoyed the ride much better than I did the town. We went by the stockyards on the Sheyenne where the trees are very beautiful. The daisies are blooming, much handsomer than we have at home, very deep orange with black centers; also goldenrod and asters.

We hired two men, one called The Kid, the other, Boyd, a deserter from Warner's Brigade. We got a letter from Nellie and a good lot of other reading. We do not have time to keep track of the faults of Cleveland and

43

Blaine though we have *Harper's Weekly*, the Chicago *Times*, and three Republican papers; also *Puck* which is so plainly illustrated it can reach the dullest brain.

AUGUST 12

Walter went to Fargo for twine—went with a double wagon. He hired a man and his wife who were traveling and land-hunting. They came from Minneapolis in a covered democrat wagon with one horse. He is French and she, Yankee, named Pascal. I guess they would as soon stop one place as another. When we first came here I saw an emigrant wagon going east bearing on one side the following inscription:

"I've left my land of happy braves,
    Who are camped round Kampeska Lake,
To visit Wisconsin's mortgaged slaves,
    And bring them west for friendship's sake."

On the opposite side were the words: "Dakota—the poor man's friend; the world's granary."

A Fargo veterinarian came out to see Geff-horse. He has been growing thin for some time. Walter examined his mouth and found that his teeth had become sharp and had cut his mouth and tongue until he was quite likely to starve to death. The doctor filed and fixed his teeth, and Walter poured oatmeal gruel

44

down him. I have been riding after the binders of which there are eight running.

AUGUST 22

Ah me, my wedding day! Thirty-seven years ago today I was married. We have fifteen in the family but the woman is a good one to work which is quite a help to me. The Pascals can stay only two or three weeks, as they want to get settled before cold weather. We had a hard shower last night which made the yard so wet that it just swam. We fear the rain will lessen the crop yield two or three bushels to the acre, for the water lodged and shelled the ripest wheat.

The sloughs are pink and white and purple with daisies; and there are yellow marigolds, great quantities of them, just in front of our door. Some of our men went down to the Sheyenne and brought back nearly a bushel of plums, very nice ones too, large and red and sweet. They are sold in Fargo for one dollar a bushel, while wheat is sixty cents. There is a perfect tangle of brush, vines, and trees to the water's edge where the fires have not destroyed them. Everything that can stand the cold grows luxuriantly in Dakota. Walter sowed turnips on the breaking which were the nicest ones I ever saw, just as smooth, and weighed four or five pounds on the average.

Potatoes, beets, cabbages, carrots—all vegetables grow large and smooth.

AUGUST 27

Geff-horse wandered off into the slough and died. They had been feeding him on a bottle and he had gotten so thin and weak that he could hardly stand. Our boys finished harvesting all the wheat and oats. McKay, who is to thresh, with his crew of twenty men, his tents, and his cook house are already on the grounds. The outfit looks very picturesque among the shocks of wheat. Many farmers are stacking and the fields are covered with shocks and stacks. The country teems with threshing machines. I could see eight this morning, each with a crew of from twenty to thirty men which makes lively times. Most farmers draw their wheat to the stockyards where they put it into cars which are shipped to Duluth. We have seven teams running. Walter flies all the time. He wants to be in several places at once.

We have been reading in a Wisconsin paper of a man and his wife and three children who left New York City last May and have walked as far as Clinton, Wisconsin, on their way to Dakota. Their household goods are loaded on a two-wheeled cart which they have drawn the entire distance, but which needed repair-

ing at this point. The man thought the far
west would be rather dangerous, so he
brought along a revolver with which to protect himself. The children's ages are nine,
seven, and four. The youngest has been drawn
part of the way, but the others have walked
every step of the distance. I hope they may
find a home nice enough to justify their hard
experience.

SEPTEMBER 2

A very heavy rain started yesterday, which
stopped all threshers. It was quite general all
over the territory. I think some one must
have prayed too hard for rain. McKays have
to board two threshing crews all through it.
They have six tents, two cook-cars, and four
cooks. Walter set some of his men to plowing, and others to moving oats from one building to another. If there is nothing else for
them to do, he will have the oats moved back
again next rainy day.

Last night a party of noted Indians were to
pass through Fargo to pose as attractions at
the Minnesota Fair. They were: Sitting Bull,
Spotted Horn Bull, Long Dog, Gray Eagle,
Flying By, Crow Eagle, Princess Winona, and
Red Spear. Most of them are Sioux chiefs.
They come from Standing Rock Agency at
Fort Yates which is out west of us on the
Missouri River.

47

The first frost. Looking from the granary steps with the telescope I could see twenty threshing machines running. The weather is perfect, and they will thresh an average of 1,500 bushels each. Walter says it is the same all over Cass County. If wheat were not so low, it would bring wealth without stint to Dakota farmers.

Fifty-five hundred bushels of grain are stored in the granary. Last night the boys who sleep there got frightened, left their beds, and came down to sleep in the barn. They say the grain cracked all night. We have 12,000 bushels of wheat, and 3,400 bushels of oats in storage here. McKay's crew threshed from the shock, and we paid them fifteen cents a bushel for threshing.

Fred started for home. He has been here steadily for two years, and I thought he ought to visit Nellie and have a little holiday. How we are to live without him I cannot say, only that we lived without Katie. The boys in the granary will miss him, for there will be no music there now. Mr. Sleeper came and took away Jack, the shepherd dog, which he left here last spring when he was digging wells. I have become very much attached to Jack, as have all the family, but Mr. Sleeper would not let us keep him.

The Fargo *Argus* reports that an unknown man tried to assassinate Sitting Bull Wednesday evening in St. Paul as he left the Opera House. The motive is thought to be revenge, and the would-be assassin is supposed to be a relative of one of the Custer Massacre victims. The frontiersmen are disgusted with the way the old Indian is being lionized. People say he would lead his braves on the warpath at the slightest provocation, scattering murder and rapine wherever he went.

SEPTEMBER 30

This is a red letter day.[1] Nellie and her cousin, Kit, came unexpectedly. They arrived at Canfield where Walter and Tom met them with a double wagon in true country style. I have had no letter from Fred but he had gotten safely home before Nellie left.

It was very warm tonight with little showers, just like spring. The grass and the tops of the vegetables are still green. About midnight I heard a rapping at the door, and upon looking out found Jack, the dog, asking to come in. He looked tired and was very hungry. I do not know how far he had come, but they had started for Minnesota.

OCTOBER 1

Willie Sleeper came again for Jack. He said

---

[1] This entry was written in red ink.

Jack had come back eighteen miles. The poor dog wanted some of his granny's bread—and he got it. I hated to have Mr. Sleeper take him. He didn't want to go. They are going directly home, so I presume I have seen the last of my good Jack.

OCTOBER 5

There was a severe thunder shower last night which kept me awake. About two o'clock I heard a familiar tapping at the outside door. I hurried down and there stood my poor, good Jackie, all bedraggled with mud, and so tickled to see me and get home that he nearly wagged his tail off. There was a piece of large, new rope hanging to his neck which I suppose he had gnawed off after they had left him for the night. Walter has tried in vain to buy him; but I have him yet.

This afternoon Sleeper came after Jack who was nowhere to be found. They should not have left him until he became so attached to me. Our little nigger cat, that we all thought so much of, met with an accident last night. Either one of the sharp tools or an old cat put her eyes out and we had to have her shot.

OCTOBER 9

The sharp frost seems to have cleared the sky of clouds and it is very beautiful. These are glorious yellow days, which show there is an Indian summer in Dakota. We have only one spare horse and buggy, and the horse is always one that is unfit for work—except when Walter is obliged to keep a good one off the plow to go to Fargo—so the girls can go out only two at a time which is rather unpleasant. But then, we are here to work.

OCTOBER 14

A bright, warm day. Yesterday the girls wore winter cloaks to Fargo; today they are out without wraps. Nellie and Katie have gone to the Hayes farm with Walter and John to get a load of turnips. Kit prefers to ride on the gang plow, Eugene McAuliffe walking close beside her so there is no danger.

The men brought in a turnip from the field that weighed twelve pounds and was thirty inches in circumference. Walter saw a cabbage head on exhibition in Fargo that weighs thirty-four pounds and is four feet, six inches in circumference. It is to be sent to the New Orleans exposition. If we had a good cellar to store our vegetables we would be well fixed, but our cellar is full of water. Dry wells and wet cellars seem to be a feature of this country.

Who can tell what an hour may bring forth? The team behind Kit ran away, becoming frightened at the discharge of a gun, and knocked her from the plow. We were very much alarmed and thought surely she was killed. As it was, she had a narrow escape from injury, if not death. She has some bruises and is badly shaken up, so much so that she fainted after walking to the house. I had forbidden her riding on the plow, but the boys and girls had overruled my objections. She will not wish to do so again, and I am thankful that she was not hurt more.

OCTOBER 18

Two years ago today we arrived at the Dodge farm. They have been short years to me for I have had plenty to do. I have enjoyed my life here very much and have never wished to leave. The girls are sewing, crocheting, ironing, and visiting, and so passing the time, which is very pleasant to me. Evenings they make molasses candy and invite in the farm hands. The boys are gentlemanly and nice. We are never troubled with them for they never stop a minute in the house unless invited.

I read in the paper the following story about Dakota's popular new governor: "Last week Governor Pierce with a party of friends took a trip down the Missouri River to Fort Yates where one hundred braves and two hundred squaws danced for them, and a handsome reception was given them by the officers. The oldest and most truthful settlers were made to relate how the favorite recreation on steamers in early times was shooting Indians; and how the buffaloes crowded so thickly into the river that the deck hands had to pull them on board to secure a passage through them." The early settlers must have had thrilling experiences by water as well as by land.

OCTOBER 24

The ground is covered with snow and the air is as cold as winter. I went out before daylight with a candle to look at the thermometer and found it six above zero. Nellie started home, Walter taking her to Fargo. Kit will stay a few days longer, but she is homesick and I fear she will not enjoy herself. It is rather late for a visit to Dakota, for the winds are too sharp and unpleasant to be out of doors. Walter brought a limb of bananas which Theron sent from Kansas City. He also brought the letters, among them one from Fred to his mother. Fred's letters are rare from their scarcity, like gold. They are never long, but they are very dear to me.

NOVEMBER 4

Today is the great national election and what a lot of excitement will prevail over all the land! The boys have gone to Fargo where they will remain in the theatre to hear the election bulletins read.

Miss Phelps called here today. She and her sister came to the territory three years ago, almost without means. They have been trading city lots and taking up claims and are now worth a great deal of money. They think that any energetic, self-reliant young lady could find no place where she could do so well as in this territory.

It was very dark last night and so foggy that one could scarcely see an inch from his nose. Somebody was lost on the prairie south of here. We could hear him halloo for two hours, but as there were houses in that direction our folks did not go to his assistance. It was not cold enough to freeze anyone. We hung out lights but it is difficult to see them in a fog.

NOVEMBER 12

Another bright day. I washed the flannels and calicoes, 'twas such a nice day for drying. Two years ago we were having a terrible blizzard. One would have a different opinion of Dakota this fall. I went with Walter across the plowing to the Hayes place which gave me a good shaking up, but then, I was out for pleasure. The school closed today and there will be no more until spring. Last winter the attendance was so small that it was thought advisable to have no winter school.

Sixteen degrees below zero. We were hardly prepared for such a cold snap. We have two men left, and if one of them were only Fred how glad I would be! The men came in from the granary tonight. Too much wood is required to keep them warm there evenings, and the wind blows so hard that we are afraid of fire. I was out around the yard today but the ground was bare, and there were great, ugly cracks which were so large that one could put in a broom stick, full length.

I copied this from the Fargo *Argus:* "A gentleman, having been snowed in on Thanksgiving in a Dakota town, was invited to go to church. He accepted, and heard the deacon make the following prayer: 'O Lord, we thank thee that our crops have not yielded us loss, but we would earnestly pray for better prices for wheat. And we pray thee, O Lord, that thou would'st protect us against false inspection at the elevator. Thou knowest the price of wheat, O Lord, and we beseech thee to see that Brother Smith's men do not misinform us. We know the value of wheat, O Lord, but we pray thee to tell us what we should receive when we deliver it. Thou knowest all that is done in the elevator, but we do not, and we pray thee inform us and thy name shall have all the glory, for ever and ever. Amen.' "

Thanksgiving Day, and a lonely one for us. This is the sixth Thanksgiving that has passed since our family were all together. Three of the number are gone forever, John, Gramp, and Anna. Today I have only Walter and Katie, of my family, here, but I have roasted the turkey as ever and I feel glad that all is well.

Our horse, Billy, was sick this morning which alarmed Walter. The boys doctored him all the forenoon and had the satisfaction of seeing him better by noon. He is a very cunning horse. He wanted the boys to stay in his stall, and as soon as they would leave, he would groan to call them back, as though he liked to be nursed.

Walter went to the Hayes farm and got the windows there to put on over ours. Our windows have frosted so thickly for the past two winters that we could not see out at all. We cannot afford double ones until wheat is more than fifty cents.

Katie and Walter have been to Fargo to an

entertainment given for the benefit of the poor of the town. They came home by moonlight at midnight, warm and comfortable, declaring: "This weather can't be beat in *any* country." A large gray owl is flying around the house this evening. A bird of ill omen, they say.

DECEMBER 1

Such a lovely day that we washed all the granary clothes for the last time this year, eleven sheets, and pillow cases without number. What a blessing our cistern has been to us! We have never been out of soft water since Walter put it down, and we have even furnished our neighbors with some. There is always plenty of work and we get no time to sew except a little in winter. I cannot see to sew evenings.

There happened a change in the program today, the boys splitting wood instead of drawing hay. Our cows ran off and, as it was snowing hard, we could not find them last night. This morning was clear and Walter soon discovered the cows, with the spyglass, way down on the Sheyenne. Without a telescope we might not have found them for a week.

DECEMBER 4

I was sick all day yesterday. Walter brought me Cherry Pectoral, Bushe's German Liniment, two bottles of medicine from the doctor, peppermint brandy; besides oranges, candy, and gum. If all this does not cure me I ought to die. It is still cloudy with the snow falling lazily now and then, which is rather unusual for Dakota. The sun shines here more than in any other country in which I have lived. It begins to seem like Dakota winter. But I am feeling better, and we can read and be quiet and comfortable, so let it come.

DECEMBER 15

Eighteen degrees below zero.

"From all this large excess of wintry gloom,
  The ungenerous sun grants us but scant reprieve."

The sun is shining but it is such a ghostly light, so white! The boys came in half frozen from their chores. Doing chores is not much fun in Dakota in wintertime. Boys used to work for their board in the East but they will not do it here, and I do not blame them. If only the sleighing were good! Anyone would be likely to freeze in a wagon.

The cold weather has cleared the air and tonight we could see eight trains of cars at once on the Fargo Southern, Manitoba, Northern Pacific, and Southwestern railways. This morning, in a mirage which would have been worth going many miles to see, the houses looked like old German castles straight out of a picture book.

The mercury goes into the ball at forty, and it is now out of sight, so we shall not know how cold the weather is. Katie is thawing the frost from the front windows with a warm flatiron so as to let in the light. A fine snow has been drifting by all day. Tonight the sun is setting with three large dogs, the like of which I never saw before. I suppose it is always so in the north. I do not believe apples or any other fruit will ever grow here. No. 1 hard wheat will be the chief product of Dakota for all time. Still, the railroad facilities are so good that people need not be deprived of fruit if they have money with which to buy it.

This is Christmas Eve. The wind howls dismally around the house. We will not be likely to hear Santa Claus' bells way out on the cold prairie where we dwell, but I have no little stockings for him to fill. The children are grown to manhood and womanhood, and scattered far apart, and their father has gone to return no more. Tomorrow I shall wish the family a Merry Christmas and give them a good dinner on this, the third Christmas I have passed in Dakota Territory.

The wind blew violently today and howled as though enraged at finding any obstacle in its path where it has had full sweep for hundreds of years. Tonight the sky is clear and the moon shines brightly on New Year's Eve. The temperature is thirty degrees below zero at twelve, midnight. The old year closes with a snap. Good-bye, Old Year.

1885

In the home of the Dakotas,
In the land of shine and sun;
Where is found surcease from sorrow
And a home for everyone;
Where the cruel blasts of winter
Scarcely ever have been felt;—
Oh, it's there our stake is driven,
In the Great Banana Belt.

# 1885

THE NEW YEAR opens cold and bright
with Walter, Katie, and myself the family,
inclusive, on the Dodge farm. We have fifteen
horses, two cows, one pig, two dogs, and two
cats. Mart went to the barn this morning and
found a new calf. I am very glad for we have
had no milk for two months. We might have
bought milk from an old lady a mile away,
but we would have had to pay eight cents a
quart for it which I could not stand with
wheat at fifty cents. Wheat is advancing in
price, but it is still too low for farmers to
raise with profit. We have counted the cost.
If the whole country were piled high with
grain, needy people would still be allowed to
starve. Poor farmers are obliged to sell,
while rich buyers can hoard, waiting for
higher prices.

This diary is a gift from Walter. It is much
too nice, for the inside will compare poorly
with the gilt outside; but that will not be the
first time such a state of things has existed
in this world.

JANUARY 4

Quite a change from forty below, yesterday,
to twenty above, today. The day is a beautiful

one and Katie and I have melted snow and washed.

Our little nigger cat has been having fits. This is the fifth one that has had them. We have had hard luck trying to raise kittens on this farm. The old nigger cat froze his ears off and Walter says he looks like a "hiller." Jack, the shepherd dog, cut his foot on the ice crust and walks on only three legs. He was helping the boys fetch in the horses. Old Roxy is so fat that she scarcely moves. She lies by the fire all day and snores.

JANUARY 10

This is the eighth pleasant, warm day. Really, Dakota is outdoing herself. Such mild weather in midwinter is scarcely ever heard of, even in Wisconsin. The horses are all out prancing. They are fat and full of life. Our cow, Daisy, gives a pailful of milk and, what do you think, we have cream in our coffee! I have made a little milk room of the closet off the sitting room. The coal stove heats it night and day, and I have a splendid chance to make butter there this cold weather. I have already churned six pounds. The price in town is thirty cents a pound. I do hope my rose geranium will not get frostbitten. Our sitting room is very sunny having one south and two west windows, though they still seem east windows to me.

The cold is stinging and the wind blows hard which means cold in Dakota, no matter what the mercury is. I hear of many people being frozen to death, but not in our immediate vicinity. Our neighbors have lived on their farms too long to get caught in that way. They took up their land seven or eight years ago, and all of them have now proved up and own their farms.

There is a young man in Fargo without hands who lost them when his parents tried to move a short distance in winter. His father took the household goods and cattle; and he took his little brothers on a hand sled. A blizzard came on and he got lost. When the father went back to find them, the oldest boy's hands were frozen stiff and both of the small children were dead. This young man keeps a news room and bookstore, and can handle his money as nimbly as anybody. It seems to me that I should want to leave a country that had proven so treacherous.

JANUARY 18

The ground is bare and the great, deep cracks look horrible to me. The other day Mart Sabin got the wheel of his wagon into one of them and had to chop it out. The crevices do not close up for ever so long, and driving is extremely dangerous unless one watches out for them.

Katie and I have shoes made of woolen braid woven basket-fashion, lined with wool in the fleece. They look like boxing gloves on Katie's small feet. We are quite protected here. Our buildings shelter somewhat on the northwest—a large granary, a horse barn, and a cow barn lie in that direction—and directly north is a large, low building for machinery. The house is a story-and-a-half high, with a long lean-to on the north side, making a kitchen and pantry. The buildings are all painted red with white trimmings. They constitute quite a respectable outfit for a Dakota farm.

Katie has twenty scholars in her school. They were all born in this vicinity, some on cold winter nights when not even a neighbor could be called in to assist the mothers; yet they are all here to tell the tale, and they are hardy specimens of Dakota. There are very few sick people in this country. We have not had to call a physician once since we came here which is fortunate as doctors charge a great deal to go into the country.

JANUARY 27

Twenty-eight below and John froze his nose, but Walter won't freeze because he is bound to think Dakota a very warm country. I am afraid he will get left some of these *warm* days when the mercury is fifty below zero. The boys started early and hauled two big loads of wheat apiece to the stock yards and huge loads of hay home, which I call a good day's work. They have to go without their dinner or eat frozen "chuck," and they were very hungry when they reached home just at dark. I had a good supper ready: boiled beef, vegetables, mince pie, doughnuts —such things as hungry men like. Walter owned, for once in his life, that he was nearly bushed. (That expression will not apply on our Dakota farm where there is not a bush on the whole two sections.) There are large numbers of sheep in the stockyards and, in summer, a post-office named Haggart. I watch with the spyglass when they are working there, and when they begin to load for the homeward trip, I begin to prepare supper.

JANUARY 29

We have been alone all day with the exception of a call from Harry Green who is a Canadian and therefore does not mind the weather. Many Canadians live around here, and they seem to endure the cold much better than we do. Eight miles from us is a French settlement called "Holy Cross" where, people tell me, there are lovely gardens and flowers in great abundance. The spot must be a sheltered one, for the wind has torn my pansies to tatters both seasons. The ones which *did* live were immense. A book agent called who is canvassing Dakota on foot selling *The Life of Garfield* and an illustrated *Testament*, both rather old. I am reading *Hyperion*.

FEBRUARY 2

People say it is six years since there has been an open winter like this. Before six o'clock Katie and I had our washing flying from the lines where it has been all day in the bright sun. The day has been lovely even to the end, so still and warm it seems almost ominous.

Tonight, just at dark, a machine agent drove up who wanted to stop over night with us. We could not refuse although we do not like to keep strangers. He says his name is Howland, and his native place is Racine, Wisconsin.

FEBRUARY 5

The snow in this country never seems to fall, but goes straight by, for there is nothing to break the breeze which, even though it may not be very brisk, carries the snow along. Under the Green Mountains where I was brought up, and in Kingston, there was timber close by. Here, the world is wide and there is not a stick or shrub on the whole farm of more than a thousand acres.

Everything is covered with snow. The little silver-breasted birds are around in great numbers. The ground is literally alive with them. They fly up at the least noise, but soon settle again to their seeds. They seem tame and come close to the house. I mean that they shall be fed all winter. I think they must crawl into the stacks at night, for there is no other shelter, and they are here as soon as daylight appears.

Roxy tries to follow Walter about the place, but she soon runs to the house and fairly screams with the cold. Being old, she likes to lie in her box a great deal. Jack follows the boys to the hayfields and all around the premises, but although he seems to know by appearances when they are going to Fargo, he never offers to go with them.

I got up the other night thinking the moon shone unusually bright and, on looking out, saw three moons, the two false ones nearly as bright as the real one. Each had a bright streak, like the tail of a comet, reaching down to the horizon in the west. I never saw anything like it before.

FEBRUARY 10

Thirty-two degrees below zero. Mr. Keenan came out from Fargo. He was very cold, indeed, having no buffalo coat. No other will keep out the cold of this country where the wind sweeps so fiercely across the open prairie. Mr. Keenan has been here several times. He said he got hungry. (There's many a true word spoken in jest.)

We sold the white cow for beef as she was a kicker. The horses have killed about half my chickens, and I have decided there is no use trying to raise them without a hen house. We have such quantities of screenings that I wish I had a hundred hens. There is no better market for eggs in America. I think some enterprising people might get rich in this business. Now that wheat is so low, farmers should turn their attention to some other industry.

FEBRUARY 21

Walter has gone home. Fred would have come back had I asked him, but I thought the two boys would enjoy a visit there, together. Roxy hunted about the place, and rushed out when Mart came, but when she found that Walter was not with him, she crawled back in her box. Jack has stayed out on the banking and watched until late this evening.

It has been a spring day, cloudy and sunny by turns, with a gorgeous sunset. We ironed with the doors and windows open. We read of snow blockades all over the country, but there have been none here and we have hauled all our hay with wagons. In the three winters we have been here, none of the railroads have been blockaded, and I have only once or twice seen a snowplow go up on the Northern Pacific. When the companies first put the railroads through here, people thought they were crazy and called this the "Great Banana Belt" as a sarcastic epithet. But the railroad has proven a great civilizer, for besides helping to subjugate the troublesome red man, it has helped build up and make habitable the great Northwest.

MARCH 6

Grover Cleveland is now president of these United States. God grant that he may prove a good one.

The boys arrived at the farm at 2 P. M., and needless to say I was exceedingly glad to see them. Fred has grown tall since he went away. The wind has been increasing to a gale, and, as there is so little snow to fly, the dirt and straw and hay fill the air and one's eyes as well. The boys have to wear goggles. The snow comes in squalls, but I have not seen a single flake fall to the ground, and I think it must be on its way to South Dakota where I hear a few people have been seeding. We have not had a drift two feet deep on the place this winter. No doubt we will get our March weather now that we have had our April.

<br>

MARCH 16

Twenty degrees below zero. There was an eclipse of the sun at noon, and I could scarcely see to get dinner. The weather was too cold to go outside to watch it. My rose geranium chilled for the first time this winter. It measured forty inches from the soil to the topmost leaf, and was a regular tree in form. I loved it. The ink jug, bluing bottle, and other things in the kitchen and pantry froze solid.

A man named Woodin froze to death in Fargo Sunday night. While under the influence of liquor, he fell off the sidewalk and was unable to regain his feet. He was on a back street where, in the morning, he was found stiff and stark.

A traveling agent came here selling broadcast seeders set on a wagon box. Soon after he left, a book agent called with *The Lives of Cleveland and Hendricks*. We will wait until their term at Washington expires before we buy, as we might possibly be ashamed of them.

Walter bought some wood from an Englishman or a Mennonite, I don't know which, any-

<br>

way he had "hoak, halder, hash, and hellum"
to sell. I think anyone should be prosecuted
for cutting trees on the Sheyenne where there
is only a narrow strip on each side of the
river. Some folks would sell their souls for
money. Walter bought the butt of a tree that
had been completely grown over with moss,
and, although it had been split, some of the
moss still adhered to it. I brought in part of
the log and sprinkled it with water, and a
miniature forest rose up, such a bright green!
It is beautiful.

MARCH 23

The mercury is just at zero where it has been
for six successive days. The three winters we
have passed in Dakota have been as different
as possible. There has not been one blizzard
in 1885, and no snow since January. The
snow is coming today in great clouds, driving
in at every crevice, but the wind is not fierce
enough for a blizzard. I have seen several
pieces in the papers as to the derivation of the
word "blizzard," but if a person were out in
one, I think the word would occur to him even
though he had never heard it. I doubt if real
blizzards exist anywhere except on the broad,
open prairie. I read in a Wisconsin paper, of
one there. The writer watched the flakes go
"eddying by." That gave them dead away.

Flakes don't wait to eddy here. They whistle and go straight by as though shot from a cannon.

> Though we wrestle with sorrow and battle with
> pride,
> 'Tis a glorious thing to have lived and died.
> —for some people!

APRIL 4

The snow has left the ground soft and sticky. Roxy came in with her feet as large as my fist. Walter had to hold her while I washed them, for it annoys Katie very much to have the floor get muddy. Mart heard prairie hens this morning. I suppose the buds are starting on my maples in Wisconsin. If we were there, Katie would tap my big maple tree, stick in a tin funnel, and commence making maple sugar. We must not think of those things now, only of seeding, and there is little comfort in that at the present price of wheat.

APRIL 11

I am glad that we can have the same men that were here last year. They planted eighty acres yesterday which was a big day's work, as seeding is the hardest part of farming in Dakota. The men walk between eighteen and twenty miles a day besides lifting sacks, filling seeders, and managing horses; moreover it is frequently either muddy or dusty in the spring.

We have all been sick. Perhaps the water is more unhealthful in the spring. It does not seem to quench thirst. The water we use for drinking should be boiled, but we have no time to take care of ourselves. Katie has nearly trotted her feet off. Three hours brisk work are required each day to wash dishes, when we both work. Walter has wiped her dishes while I have been sick. Yesterday, when he broke a dish, he told her that the price of it would have to come out of her wages, as it was through her agency that the dish was broken.

APRIL 19

I have been out listening to the melodious song of a meadow lark as he sits on the ridge pole of the machine shed. Oh, how sweetly he does sing! It almost brings tears to my eyes. Song birds are scarce here. I have seen very few robins, none yet this spring, but the meadow lark never fails us. There is one bird that whistles, and very large flocks of the little brown ones with silver breasts which fly over the prairie. Walter says he does not believe they pick up wheat for if they did, being so numerous, they would take it all. I just heard a killdeer sing.

The slough is running, or rather, the water in the slough. It always looks as though running with the wind, rapidly. A stranger would suppose that one might drive across these prairies anywhere, but if he did not know the ground, he would quite likely fetch up in a slough. Since we came here a man drove into one of them and drowned a four-horse team.

It seems strange to think that there is an army so near us. Riel's half-breeds, with the Indians, will give the Canadian soldiers a sorry chase, we think. The half-breeds have so much wild country to fall back into and they think they have right on their side. They have been down from Winnipeg and bought all the arms and ammunition there are in Fargo.[1]

APRIL 23

A bloody conflict took place last Friday between Riel's insurgents and General Middleton's troops which brought sorrow to scores of homes in Winnipeg. I read this in the

---

[1] Louis Riel was a French-Canadian half-breed who, because of his education and powers of leadership, exercised much influence over the ignorant half-breed inhabitants of northwestern Canada in 1870. These half-breeds believed that their land was about to be taken from them. Riel led the settlers in revolt and troops were sent to quell the rebellion. Riel was officially banished from Canada for five years and fled to Montana.

In March, 1885, Riel was taken back from the United States by his countrymen to assist them in obtaining redress of certain grievances. Revolt broke out and the Indians immediately went on the warpath, murdering and pillaging the settlers. Forces of Mounted Police and five thousand troops under General Middleton were sent against them. Riel was soon captured, and Big Bear, the Indian leader, fled to the fastnesses of the prairie wilderness.

*Argus:* "Canada's little war is doing for Dakota and Montana on a small scale what many people hoped to see an Anglo-Prussian war do for the whole country at large. Horses, hay, oats, and other supplies for the Canadian troops in Saskatchewan are being bought in large quantities on this side of the border, and if Riel holds out long, the demand is likely to increase. It's an ill wind that blows no good to somebody in this great Republic."

Mrs. Griffin came running over today with the news that Joe Moran was dead. They had consulted a doctor who had called the disease typhoid fever. Joe was delirious most of the time. Walter and John went down and made the poor boy's last toilet. The family seemed almost wild with grief, none of them having been in bed the long night through. They expressed their feelings with loud lamentations and cries, with no attempt at control. The Morans had sent for a priest but he did not arrive until after Joe was dead. So the boy died without shrift, but he had gone to confession at Easter. I cut leaves enough from my rose geranium to make a wreath for his coffin, and Katie added some white daisies which made it look quite well. Joe had a claim at Devil's Lake which he broke last fall. He was to go there this summer to occupy it and be married in the fall.

Walter and Fred have gone to the funeral. Farmers are very busy but somebody must bury the dead. I had never seen a funeral procession in Dakota before. It was in sight over an hour and looked very picturesque winding its tedious way over the prairie.

Mr. Dodge writes that he would like to have a rise in the price of wheat but not at the expense of a war between England and Russia which is threatened and seems almost inevitable. I think the sentiments of western people generally are expressed in the following lines which I found in the New York *World:*

> The Lion and the Bear are growling,
>   How stand the crop?
> For while the dogs of war are howling
>   Our wheat goes up.

MAY 1

Walter went out this morning and brought in some tiny yellow buttercups, carrying them to Katie before she was up. It is too cold to go a-Maying. I suppose my tulips are up at home; however there is no country but affords some comfort to the dwellers therein. Our wheat begins to show and will soon look like a waving green ocean, and the little buttercups, which have come without the aid of human hands, have a smell of spring which no tulip, ever so sweet, can outdo.

> Darling little buttercups blossoming alone,
> The last snowdrift is scarcely gone
> Ere your tender buds have blown.

The maples that I brought from home have all died, but one that was covered has some sprouts coming up from the roots. Box elders, which are perfectly hardy, are the best to grow here, on the open prairie. When we first came here dealers in trees could be found at every station on the railroad, doing a heavy business, too. Box elder and ash seed sold for three dollars per bushel.

MAY 10

The boys brought home four little foxes and put them in a box. They have somehow escaped; but when we put out food they carry it off. They play around the machinery, looking very cunning. I hope they will go away soon, for they are almost large enough to catch my hens.

The wind has blown everything to pieces that has come in my seven by nine flower garden. I always had flowers at home, so I feel that I must have at least a few pansies.

The sky cleared at sunset. First we saw a light streak in the north which widened rapidly, the clouds all flying southward, finally reaching the place the sun was setting. The sun looked like burnished gold, and threw its rays into the flying black clouds which kept ever on their way southward. In less than an hour the sky was perfectly clear. I never saw anything so grand. When night came on the stars shone with great brilliancy, and the new moon looked glad and gay.

MAY 18

It has been a terrible day, the wind blowing so hard that the boys could hardly see to plow. They said all the soil seemed to be in the air at once. A whirlwind will take up the dust and whirl it across the whole section. I should suppose it would suck up the wheat, which is not growing as yet. Nobody at home would think of working out of doors on such a day, but we have to rustle here, where we put in so much wheat and have it in as early as possible. Walter has painted "No Smoking" with a death's head and crossbones on the barn. I should think that would be effective.

MAY 23

The wind blows all the time, so hard that one can scarcely stand before it. We cannot open the front door for if we should, the room would soon be empty. I am not sure the coal stove would be left although it is a big one.

80

Katie brought me some mignonette plants from town. I have kept them covered until they are yellow, and now the wind is whipping them to shreds. There has been lightning the past two nights with a little rain, but the wind blows on just the same.

About four o'clock the sky looked fearful, we heard a distant roar, and soon the storm was upon us. The hailstones were as large as nutmegs and oh, how they did kill things! I was frightened nearly out of my wits. The peonies that I brought from home were budded for the first time, but they were cut off, tough though they be. Our wheat that looked so green has disappeared and the fields are bare. Walter says the wheat is only beaten into the ground and will come up again.

MAY 31, SUNDAY

The wheat is rising out of the ground. The day is very beautiful and I have been out nearly all of it picking posies. The air is soft and cool. I think there is something fascinating about gathering wild flowers, strolling along, not knowing what you will find. It gives one a childish delight. There is a bright yellow flower in bloom now which looks like a Montana verbena, except in color, and is as fragrant; and there are violets in great numbers, some of them nearly pink. Katie says that down at the Sheyenne the air is fragrant with blossoms. Yet I should not like to live there, for the storms follow the river and the mosquitoes are troublesome.

The river woods are looking green. I stand at the east chamber window—which is my observatory—with the spyglass every day and look at them. They seem as near as Vince's woods at home. There is only a narrow strip, but they are dense and filled with a thicket of underbrush, all tangled together. This has been cleared out in several places and farm houses stand close to the river. Hundreds of pounds of hops, growing wild, are gathered there by the settlers every year. Hops possess the qualities of yeast-making in a high degree. I think this is rightly called the land of bread—the wheat, the yeast, the water, and the coal—the very "staff of life."

JUNE 3

It is hard to cook without vegetables, but I have learned to make use of dried fruits. I put in just enough water to swell the berries, then cool them before putting in the sugar, and they swell to their full size. I make all the bread myself. We like good bread and butter at every meal. I have made all the pies since we came here with the exception of lemon pies which Katie makes better than I.

Walter is painting the sitting room floor. It is useless to try to keep a carpet here. I never believed in making a parlor out of a sitting room where members of the family should feel free to come and go as they please.

I have cut out the dress which Nellie sent me so as to finish it before Daniel arrives. Were I farther west, I should not dare to make it "Mother Hubbard" as the paper says that in Pendleton, Oregon, that type of costume is prohibited unless worn belted. Bills to that effect have been posted in the town, ladies who violate the ordinance being fined heavily. The alleged reason is that such garments "scare horses, cause accidents, and ruin business."

JUNE 7, SUNDAY

There was a terrific thunder and wind storm last night. The boys said the roof of the granary fairly wiggled, and the plows were positively blown out of the furrows. The wind tore my lovely pansies all to pieces, and the leaves on the trees hang in ribbons. Afterward, there was a hard frost which left the ground white. At half past nine this morning the ice was not all out of the watering troughs. The peonies froze so hard that the buds hung limp—what few had not been cut off.

The boys at the granary have callers as they often do on Sunday. It seems to be a novelty to the neighbor boys to come here, almost as good as going to town. The men live in a large room in the granary, and none of us women go there except on Mondays to change and air and make the beds.

I have been thinking of home and my absent loved ones today for some unknown reason. Perhaps it is because we did not get our mail on Saturday. If we only lived where we could get our mail twice a week! I sometimes get very uneasy and try to invent some excuse for Walter to go to town.

JUNE 10

Poor Roxy is getting so blind that she can see Walter but a little way off. She thinks more of him than of the rest of the family. She travels so slowly now that he seldom lets her follow him except when he goes about the place in the buggy. It almost killed her when John died. She is practically human.

Walter brought a girl from Fargo who is "seven months from Norway." If she had as good judgment as Roxy I should be glad, but she says "yes" to everything, so I cannot tell whether she understands or not. We have been mending sacks. Have patched sixty-one. They laugh at me because I call them "bags."

There has been another thunder shower with vivid lightning, the thunder roaring like cannon, and the rain pouring in torrents. The water will be fine for the gardens, but the wheat has turned a light, sickly green.

JUNE 15

There are no fences on the prairie. A few people have a small yard in which to shut their cattle at night, but most of them have a herder or picket their cattle. Our front yard is a common-sized one but back of the house, the yard extends for half a mile and is almost as wide. If it were only fenced it would be a nice piece of grass in which to let the horses run.

The fields are too wet to pull mustard which worries Walter. The men dislike weeding more than any other work; nevertheless, they have pulled all the mustard on this farm every year we have been here. They come in with their backs just wet. Fred says they have to open and shut all day like jackknives.

I found a bird's nest containing four little eggs in the grass outside our door. The bird is sitting. The meadow lark is the principal singing bird in Dakota. I have never seen a bluejay here, but they are very numerous in Wisconsin. I always love to see them for they seem so happy, even though their bonnets are a little out of style.

It is raining with some hail and one steady stream of lightning. Walter was three and a half hours coming from Fargo yesterday, the roads being almost impassable from water. Nellie writes that she went to my old home and gathered a bouquet which she placed on John's grave. I am very grateful. He should have one constantly if I were there, for he helped keep those flowers while he lived, and he was fond of them.

A neighbor sent me some rhubarb. We have none growing yet. We still make a garden on the corner of a wheatfield which is all right except that it is too far for me to run to in leisure moments, as I so love to do. The garden has been frozen, baked, and drowned, but still some of it survives. The wind has blown off everything that will come off. It is all too wet now. Walter pumped out the cellar. There is plenty of water in the three wells for the horses. We have two wooden pumps and one with a bucket and rope.

The hired girl's sister is here with her and they stay in the kitchen and jabber Norwegian. They have been singing beautifully together there this evening. Fred is reading *Hard Cash* which the rest have all read, and they discuss it to plague him, so he has gotten out his pistol for a bookmark. I have been reading *Dorcas, Daughter of Faustina.* The old black elevator hen came off with seven chickens. She had been set on fourteen eggs.

The wild roses are beginning to bloom, and I have only to go out in any direction to pick a lovely bouquet. I think wild flowers when gathered should be called nosegays, after the old-fashioned way. There are a dozen varieties in bloom near the house: three colors of spider lilies, and a purple flower that looks like a miniature Canterbury bell. A great many yellow flowers grow here, and wild roses peep out from everywhere, some light pink, some very dark crimson, and all sweet and beautiful.

We are being troubled by mosquitoes for the first time since we came here. The past week I could not keep them out of the house. Some are too large to crawl through the screens, but they come in when the doors are opened, for the grass is filled with them and so is the wheat. Walter says, coming from town the mosquitoes were as thick as bees when swarming, and the horses were almost frantic. Fred's white horse was black with them. He would wipe them off with a wisp of hay but they would not stay off a second. A day or two of hot, dry weather would will them.

My birthday, my fifty-ninth. Walter brought me a plaid gingham dress which Katie is to make for me. I wear out a calico here in four weeks. Nellie sent me a book, a birthday present.

> On the road of life one mile-stone more!
> In the book of life one leaf turned o'er!
> Like a red seal is the setting sun
> On the good and evil men have done,—
> Naught can today restore!
> —LONGFELLOW, *Sundown.*

Elsie made some very good fried cakes which is encouraging. If only she could understand English, I could teach her housework. Dakota is a lovely green now, every inch. Everybody is busy and will be in a great hurry and drive until fall plowing is done. I like farm work when there is plenty of help, indoors and out.

One great white peony is in bloom, a flower that stands this climate very well if kept covered in winter. I have just been outside and I can say that my path was strewn with roses, but if I should say my path to the pigpen, all the romance would be eliminated.

> In all places, then, and in all seasons,
> Flowers expand their light and soul-like wings,
> Teaching us, by most persuasive reasons
> How akin they are to human things.
> —LONGFELLOW, *Flowers.*

I fired a few firecrackers which smelled, at
least, like the glorious Fourth. I found three
little boys close by who had no firecrackers,
and gave them each a bunch. I have been
thinking of old times when my own children
were small. Their father always took great
pains to have them enjoy the holidays, and
had a good time with them.

Walter had a serious accident in Fargo yesterday. The horse became frightened at some
immigrant wagons and shied so suddenly that
he tipped the buggy over and then ran some
distance. Walter hung on to the lines and
was dragged on his stomach. When he let go
of the lines Dan stopped and looked around
to see what was going on.

A man was killed last night over on the
tracks near here. He had gotten drunk in
town and started to walk home on the railroad ties, when a train came along and ran
him down. The law requires an order to buy
strychnine; yet whiskey kills ten-thousand
where strychnine does one.

### JULY 30

We had a fearful storm this morning at seven
o'clock. The sky was as black as ink. Then
came the rain, wind, thunder, and lightning
with terrible force. The wind laid flat every-

thing in the garden, lodged the grain, and blew things around generally. It moved the machine house about an inch. A brood of chickens that I had taken a great deal of pains with was killed. The hen was out about two rods from the barn, too far to get in. She took the chicks under her wing, but she was blown off against the barn.

It seems strange to have Cousin Daniel here. He hitched up Gumbo, and he and Roxy and I rode around the quarter-section after supper. The daisies are blossoming in the sloughs, hundreds in one bunch: pink, purple, and white. They are about the size of a nickel. The fallen wheat and oats and vegetables have lifted. The wheat begins to have a ripe, yellow look.

AUGUST 11

Harvest has started. Now there will be no rest for man, woman, or beast until frost which comes, thank heaven, early here. I was nearly beside myself getting dinner for thirteen men, besides carpenters and tinners, with Katie sick in bed and Elsie washing. I baked seventeen loaves of bread today, making seventy-four loaves since last Sunday, not to mention twenty-one pies, and puddings, cakes, and doughnuts.

The men cut one hundred acres today. All

four of our harvesters are being used as well
as three which were hired to cut by the acre.
Things look like business with seven self-bind-
ers at work on this home section. The twine
to bind our grain will cost three hundred
dollars this year.

One of the farm hands broke the thermometer. Now if we are ever so warm we will not
know it. I shall send for one as soon as
possible.

AUGUST 16

How beautiful the wheat fields look, long
avenues between the shocks, just as straight,
one mile in length! The whole country is covered with shocks, heavy ones too. Any time
during the past week we could see a hundred
reapers with the attendant shockers—six to
four reapers. Daniel has been flying here,
there, and everywhere. Everybody is rustling,
which is what I like.

The boys have gone to the Sheyenne to see
if there are any plums. Last year there were
great quantities of them, very large for wild
ones; and grapes, large ones too. The feathery plumes of the goldenrod are beautiful,
growing everywhere. They remind me of
home. This morning one of the boys said that
this was a God-forsaken country. I told him
that the whole of Cass County was covered

with No. 1 hard wheat, and the wayside was all abloom with goldenrod and asters which proves that God has not forsaken it.

AUGUST 27

It has rained all day which has stopped the work of the threshers but not their eating. Many farmers suffer from the effects of wet weather, boarding threshing crews, hating to disband them lest they could not be assembled when needed. Crowds of men are standing around, as many as one would see in Kingston on election day. Cousin Daniel says there is a divine providence against which it is wrong to rebel. But we all seem to be rebels by nature, and I do not think it wrong to be angry when the rain wets the wheat in threshing time.

Four men took refuge in a barn during a thunder storm yesterday, five miles from here. Lightning struck the barn, killing two of them outright, and stunning the other two. One of them is still unconscious.

Our nigger cat has seven kittens which I hope to raise, every one, for they are needed about the buildings to hunt the mice that eat the sacks and bedding in the granary. The boys have a hammock and swing out there, but soon every available space will be filled with grain.

Just at noon a gentleman and lady drove to the farm to see Cousin Daniel. I was not particularly glad to see them stop for dinner.

I can see seven threshing machines running near here. The paper stated that a Casselton merchant stood on the steps of his store Tuesday morning and counted fifty-three steam threshers all at work turning out No. 1 hard wheat. Walter is everywhere. He does not get in to eat his supper until nine o'clock. Our supper table stands for two or three hours now, during threshing. The men on the three teams that are hauling from the machine cannot come in until the machine stops. Neither can Walter nor Fred. The four stackers and two plow-boys do not like to wait, so they eat at half past six, while the machine runs as long as the men can see.

The prairie is illuminated every night with burning straw. It seems wicked to burn straw. I used to have trouble to get enough to cover my roses at home. When somebody invents a machine to convert straw into fuel he will be mighty rich; however, Edison says it requires as much ingenuity to make money out of an invention as it does to make the invention.

93

A lovely, warm day with a mild, little breeze. Walter went out this morning with his overcoat on and came in, in his shirt sleeves. They finished all threshing at 4 P. M. We had 12,-000 bushels of wheat. The hot weather when the wheat was in the milk or dough caused the loss of about 2,000 bushels. The oats are very good, amounting to 30,000 bushels, or about 60 bushels to the acre.

Walter came home with a new man named Bill Miller who had come into Fargo from a farm where he had worked through harvest and threshing, earning sixty dollars. He started drinking, went to bed at the Minnesota House, and in the morning found that he had not one cent. Somebody had gone through his clothes in the night. Half of the money that is earned in Dakota goes in that manner, and the poor boys work so very hard to earn it. The northern lights gleam out tonight brighter than I ever saw them in Wisconsin.

SEPTEMBER 24

Last night I sat up from eleven until two watching the eclipse. It was a lovely night, no clouds nor wind and such a subdued, shadowy light over all. I could not enjoy it alone, so I called Walter and Katie to see it. Fred would not arouse himself, though it shone on the bed where he lay.

It is a warm, dry day, and we are very much afraid of fire. The papers report one running near Buffalo; also one at Bismarck destroying stacks, houses, and barns. People say fire was never known to run in stubble so before, nor in the prairie grass which still looks quite green.

We have been reading in a Dakota paper the account of the burning to death of a young man not many miles from here. He was out fighting the fire when it overtook him. He tried in vain to beat out the flames, but they caught in his clothing and before help could reach him he was dead. The inquest was held at ten o'clock at night out on the open, burning prairie, and the scene was the subject for a painter. On every side the prairie fire shed a lurid light, with a canopy of smoke across a blood-red moon. The jurors with uplifted hands took the oath over the body of the victim, while in the background were the witnesses, some of them on Indian ponies, making a weird and picturesque scene. He was a much-respected young man, and his terrible fate will cast a gloom over us as long as our evening skies are lighted by the fires sweeping around us.

Yesterday a fire started running while our

boys were plowing, and in ten minutes they were plowing in front of it. If the teams had not been already hitched up, it would have gotten to our buildings, for the flames reached almost to the grass. We were awfully frightened. One stack was close to the fire and not far from the house. Mr. Hanks had set it three miles away while burning straw. He says the flames jumped a wide strip of plowing, the wind carrying them over. He followed with his plow but was unable to gain control of the fire.

SEPTEMBER 27

The boys are digging in the cellar. The walls cave in as fast as they dig out the dirt, but there are now two sides planked so they have a good start at last. Yesterday the dirt caved in and knocked Walter down. The dirt is exceedingly heavy and cracks and comes off in great cakes. Later, Fred was in the cellar alone. I called him out to dig some carrots, whereupon the dirt caved in with a loud crash and with enough force to have killed him or injured him badly. Walter wants to get the cellar ready for the potatoes.

This morning the air was so smoky we could hardly breathe indoors or out; but at ten the sun began showing through the fog and smoke as red as blood. Soon, the wind came up and cleared it all away. I have some pansies that are very handsome, great purple and yellow and bronze-colored beauties. They grow much larger here than at home.

<br>

OCTOBER 2

The house is filled with smoke this morning. The air is heavy, and it is three weeks since we had rain. The burning straw and prairie fires together fill the whole country with smoke. I am reminded of home when Chicago was burning. Barney Griffin is threshing and a spark flew into a stack of wheat. In a minute it was all ablaze. The boys hurried over and drew off the separator and engine, and pitched off one stack, but the rest of the setting all burned. Poor Barney, he can ill afford the loss! This makes three times this year our boys have turned out to fight fires.

Our ground is all plowed, but there are about forty acres near us, mostly back or north of the buildings, in which stand all our haystacks. If the fire should get inside, we would all burn out. Nothing could save us. The fire ran along the Northern Pacific tracks last night so that the train did not dare pass the slough bridge. The grass is tall in the sloughs now, four feet high, and they are perfectly dry. A fire could follow there for miles. At times the smoke is perfectly suffocating.

97

OCTOBER 11

The whole country is settling down to regular fall plowing. Harvesters and threshers are leaving and soon even the plowmen will be gone. There is nothing much for men to do in Dakota in winter. Only a few laborers are needed on the farms to care for the stock.

Fred consulted Dr. Wier who says the itching from which he is suffering is the result of water or climate or something found only in the Red River Valley of the Northwest. It is quite prevalent in and around Fargo. Fred sits in the sun all day and looks miserable, and I am miserable to see him. I am afraid he will have to go through life with poor health like his father before him.

The sun came up like a great ball of fire this morning, for prairie fires still rage. The sky was all aglow at sunset. The clouds were the most beautiful I have ever seen: waves and stripes of gold, scarlet, and turquoise. Just above the eastern horizon, the heavens were purple turning to black as the sun went down. I thought it was surely going to rain; but, as night came on, the air grew cold, the moon gleamed silvery, and the stars came out in all their shining beauty.

OCTOBER 20

I cannot see that my Freddie improves. If he does not get well soon I shall propose going home with him. A change might stop his itching at least. Many are having Red River fever as well as Red River itch. The doctor said he had never heard of a case east of St. Paul. Fred has lost fifteen pounds. I am very nervous to have him sick way out here on the prairie with winter coming on when there are many days that we cannot get to town.

We have kept no coal fire yet although we have started one several times. It is almost too warm to sleep near one. We have coal from the western land near the Missouri River where there are great quantities of it. I read in an old paper about a man who took a claim west of Bismarck. While excavating for his cellar he struck a vein of lignite coal. He completed his excavation, built his house, and now, when his fire needs replenishing, he simply goes down cellar and picks loose what coal he needs. People think there is enough coal in that section to supply the whole territory, however thickly it may be populated.

Jack went away last night and came back in a terrible fix. He is all bitten up and lame in three of his legs. But he *will* fight. My rose geranium grew so tall that I could not set it in the window. So at last I had to cut it back. I was sorry to cut back a tree—the only one on the place—but I could not lift such a large plant about this winter. The red geranium and fuchsia look especially nice now that there is no green thing to be seen on the prairie.

Elsie Lessing was here for awhile. Walter hitched up Cripes so that she and Katie could go to Moran's after butter. Elsie is plowing for her father, a stingy old German who makes the women work out of doors. He thinks an hour long enough for them to prepare a meal, and affords them only the necessities of life, though he owns a half section of land with live stock and machinery. There are eight children who, with the mother, do all the work. Last spring Fritz, the oldest boy, ran away from home, thinking he had gotten too big to be whipped—he was six feet tall. He went off, out of the vicinity for awhile, and then returned to work at Green's, three miles from home, where he has been all the fall, plowing. His family have not found him yet. He works in sight of home, and can see his sister plowing, and she can see him, but she doesn't dream who he is. I think that's fun!

Plowing is a never-ending job in Dakota. As soon as threshing is finished and the crop is off the land, all the men and teams commence to plow. In the spring, after seeding, they do the summer-fallow plowing and back-setting which continue until haying begins. We can never go anywhere because we have only one horse at a time off the plow and that one is usually tired. For a week the nights have been too fearfully dark to be out anyway. One would surely be lost on the prairie. The soil is very black and with so much of it plowed, the whole earth seems covered as with a funeral pall. Tonight a large prairie fire burns off south of us. It shines on the clouds and illuminates the buildings which only intensifies the outer darkness.

> Life is a struggle and 'tis better so,
> Who treads its stormy steep, its stony ways,
> And breasts its wintry blasts must battling go,
> And yet it hath its Indian summer days.

NOVEMBER 5

The dark, cloudy weather continues with neither sun by day nor moon by night. It is so dark we can scarcely see in the kitchen. The thermometer stays at thirty-two. But the plowing goes steadily on which is the main thing. If Fred gets much thinner I shall not dare let him go out. The Dakota winds blow hard. He has been rather lonesome since he has been sick. Walter brought him a box of cigars, though Walter never smokes himself, nor makes use of any intoxicating drink, thank God!

Campbell and Billy are banking the house, Mart and Charles (whom the boys call Calamity) are killing a pig, and Walter is working at both jobs alternately. It seems a pity to have only one hog on this big farm, for hogs do well here on wheat that is kept in soak—or on screenings, rather. But unless a good, warm pen is afforded them, they won't winter well here. Walter cut up the pork which weighs three hundred pounds.

There is a small mountain of manure behind the barn which Walter thinks will benefit the crop. He is having it put on a piece of land which he intends to summer-fallow next year. A dark cloud hangs around the horizon and it looks like spring.

NOVEMBER 16

It stormed all night. This morning the ground is covered with snow which looks much better than the bare, black earth. The fall plowing is undoubtedly ended. Two Dutch peddlers came here today. We traded a little just to encourage them to go on breaking roads.

Walter has been patching, puttering, and puttying about the barn windows. Katie and I have melted snow and washed. We had ten sheets and innumerable other things. Twenty-two towels is our usual number. We had just hung the clothes out when the wind began to blow. We had to bring them in and dry them around the kitchen fire. Everybody knows what a delightful job that is!

We are tormented with mice which gnaw everything in the house. When Katie last went to Fargo, she took down her silk cloak which hung in the closet, and found a mouse's nest in the sleeve. Mice had eaten a hole in the material and pulled out the batting of which to make the nest.

Walter bought a pair of long-legged boots which suit him very well. I was not sure but that he would sleep in them as Theron did his first pair. The evenings are becoming very long, and although we have supper after dark, there is a long time to sit and read. We have *Harper's Monthly* and *Weekly*, the Milwaukee *News*, New York papers, the *Examiner*, the *Argus*, besides others which Walter buys at the news room.

I suppose Louis Riel was hanged today in Canada; but I am afraid that will not end the insurrection.[1]

NOVEMBER 22

A fine mirage this morning. We could not see Fargo, but could see miles beyond it. That

---

[1] Riel was tried in Regina in July, sentenced to death, and executed on November 10, 1885. For some time after his death other leaders attempted to rouse the half-breeds to further rebellion, but they, as well as the Indians, realized the power of the Canadian Government, and from that day to this peace has prevailed in that western country.

city lies so close to the river that the trees hide it. There is almost always a cloud of car smoke over it. Two electric lights replace the one that blew down in Fargo last summer. The towers are not nearly as tall as the other, but they are plainly visible above the trees on the Sheyenne. The night we arrived in Dakota, an Englishman on the train was watching for the town and when he saw this light exclaimed, "Ah, that looks like a stah of the fi'st magnitude!"

NOVEMBER 26

Thanksgiving Day. This used to be a day of unusual gladness, for on this day Walter was born, and he has proved a great blessing to me. We used to try, after the fashion of New Englanders, to be all at home on Thanksgiving if it were possible. I have been very happy with my family around the table many years —how happy, I did not realize until that sad day on which the father was taken from us and I was left alone with the children. Never since then have all the children been with me on this day. It is our fourth Thanksgiving in Dakota. The turkey is roasted and eaten, and the day has gone; I am thankful.

DECEMBER 1

The snow began falling in true New England fashion about eight o'clock this morning. It

Katie Woodward

Fourteen Binders at Work on a Bonanza Wheat Farm

Seeders Sowing No. 1 Hard

Mortie Woodward, One of the "Two Good Grandchildren"

snowed for two hours and then grew so warm the snow turned to rain, and oh, my soul, how nasty it is! Elsie and Lena Lessing came riding at full speed without a saddle all over the prairie, reminding me of the old riddle: "Without a saddle, I ride astraddle."

Walter has been shipping his wheat to Duluth. A carload was shipped from Lisbon on Thanksgiving Day. When it arrived in Duluth the grain inspector found the body of a man in it. He had been killed in the car with a coupling pin and it was bespattered with his blood. They called a doctor and the sheriff who found $475 in his pocket. For this, he had evidently been killed, but the murderer had not found the money. He was apparently a hard working man who had started home with his money. Somebody had known of it who had wanted the money badly enough to commit such a deed. Thank heaven, he didn't get it, and if he is never found out he must carry the deed on his conscience which will be punishment enough.

Later. We have just heard that the man who was murdered in the car of wheat was a Norwegian from Tower City who had just sold his claim for $1,000. Part of the money was paid him in gold, which the murderer must have taken from his pockets. They have no clews as yet.

Sixteen degrees below zero at noon. The wind cuts across the prairie so sharply that it is dangerous to be out far from the house, and even Jack, the dog, cannot stay out long at a time. My house plants look comforting, now that there is nothing else green to be seen. We have only one man besides Mart, Jake Solomon, a Norwegian, a silent man. But we have hired him to take care of the barns and horses, and for that business he seems capable and sufficient.

Katie and I have one drift of snow left and we have melted some of it and washed. The wind blew me down when I went out, but I came in and took a dose of laudanum. Ha! We are neither of us strong enough for the task we have undertaken; but many a weakling before us has performed a job which was too hard for him. Walter bought ten volumes of Chamber's *Encyclopedia*. Fred is reading *Waverly or 'Tis Sixty Years Since*.

DECEMBER 13

We have been reading all day, all of us including Mr. Roberts, the teacher of our school, who also comes week-days and reads until bedtime. Besides him, we have not many visitors now that winter has come. Walter is reading *Memorie and Rime* by Joaquin Miller, and Fred, *The Wandering Jew* which Walter found in a bookstore in Fargo. He also brought *Winning His Way* which we had all read except Katie and Fred when it was first published in *Our Young Folks* the year Fred was born. There were also the Christmas numbers of *Harper's*, *The Graphic*, and *Frank Leslie's*, besides all the other papers. Walter is a great hand to buy books and papers as was his father.

Katie went over to stay at Green's last night. It seems strange to have her gone, for she has not been away from home after dark for over a year. I wonder that she is not more discontented, having always before lived in town. We are too far from town to go to any places of amusement, for in winter the weather is too cold to be out after dark. It costs too much to go to Fargo and remain over night, otherwise the children might go to the theatre occasionally. Our folks tried to go when we first came here but soon decided that it didn't pay. The house was so lonesome in the night that I could not sleep. Both clocks ran down. Katie has wound the clocks ever since her father died.

DECEMBER 17

Katie, Walter, and Fred went to Fargo in the sleigh. They brought me letters from Isabinda, Theron (the first in several months), and Nellie. Katie brought me Mrs. Heman's *Poems*, beautifully bound; and Fred brought a handsome glass bowl. They were Christmas presents but would not keep. Fred bought Walter a sealskin cap, and Walter bought Fred a buffalo coat. Fred has concluded to go home. He is taking half a dozen books for children in Kingston, and they are all sending presents to Nellie. I thought if he *would* go, he had better start before a storm came on.

It has been a beautiful day. The Kingston *Spy* says that the weather in Wisconsin has been cold, and that they have had a blizzard, which I know is not true. Let them see one of ours and they will know what a blizzard means. We had eight the first winter, but none last winter, at least not one real one.

DECEMBER 24

The ground was studded with diamonds of frost this morning, the whole yard of twenty acres gleaming and taking on lovely colors in the sunlight. The snow falls gently, great flakes sailing by as they used to in Vermont. But the winter cannot be long now. This is Christmas Eve. Walter, Katie, and I are alone.

DECEMBER 25

The mercury fell thirty degrees last night which seems to be the style in Dakota. Nellie's package contained presents for all of us: a photo album and beautiful nightgown for me; slippers and an embroidered handkerchief for Katie; for Walter, two hemstitched linen handkerchiefs; and for Fred, a pair of mittens and a scarlet silk handkerchief with his initials embroidered in yellow silk. Katie and I each received a very elegant fringed Christmas card from Eugene McAuliffe.

The day has been cold and windy and not a very merry Christmas at the Dodge farm. No sound of joyous Christmas bells on the lone prairie where we dwell. Tonight the wind howls dismally and we sit close to the fire, we three, where we will be found for many nights to come. It is not the being here on a night like this that makes one feel so lonely, but the knowing that, in any case, one could not get away.

DECEMBER 31

The last day of the year is passing, a bright, beautiful one, too. There has been no blizzard in Dakota in 1885. Nor have I been absent a day nor a night during the year. This is rather a lonely evening. Katie is not well and Walter sits reading. I have been to many a watch meeting when I was young, but never one so still as this. A certain sadness always seems to attend the closing of a year. But no

matter how we feel about it, 1885 will go
down in its place between the years that have
passed and those that are to come.

> Make haste, Old Year, you're slow, Old Year,
>   You're getting stiff and old,
> Your brothers lie all silently
>   Along the naked wold.

1886

The chinchbug eats the farmer's grain,
The bee-moth eats his honey,
The bedbug fills him full of pain,
The humbug scoops his money.

# 1886

THE FOURTH YEAR on the Dodge farm
finds us with a small family. Fred goes away
with the birds and we only hope that, like
them, he may return in the spring. We have
very few callers except Mr. Roberts. There
are three families near us, kind Irish people,
but they are not like our own old friends at
home. They seem to hold themselves rather
aloof. The sun has shone brightly all day as
have the two bright dogs that follow it, which
we think are a sign of cold weather.

Walter is making out his yearly report.
Katie is knitting herself a hood. There is a
blossom on my fuchsia which measures six
inches from the stem that joins it to the shrub
to the tip of the stamen. I never before saw
one so large. The scarlet geranium is beautiful and comforting, but if by any mishap the
coal fire should go out, good-bye plants and
blossoms. Tonight I shall have to bring everything that will freeze into the dining room.
Horses will not face the wind in a storm.

JANUARY 5

Walter and Katie have gone to Fargo in the
buggy. I am alone except for my two good
dogs: Roxy, who is so fat and old she can

scarcely walk, and Jack, the beautiful shepherd, who would tell me very quickly if anyone were approaching. The weather is extremely cold, and in spite of a good fire, we had to fetch our breakfast into the sitting room. I cooked it with my hood, shawl, and mittens on. We have the warmest house in this vicinity. It is clapboarded, sheeted, and papered; then studding is put on inside of that, onto which ship-lath, plaster, and inside paper are nailed, making seven thicknesses. Many families on this prairie have not as good houses as our kitchen. Katie said she wished she had some of the youngsters piled behind our big coal stove where the two dogs lie. She and I have shoes made of wool, and we are so bundled up that we can scarcely move, while many go poorly clad.

The boys keep busy with sixteen horses to feed and water. An abundance of water is needed for the stock. But the wells are so deep and the pumps work so hard that I cannot possibly pump a pailful. The ground is bare and covered with great, abysmal cracks which are caused, I presume, by shrinkage due to the deep freezing of the earth.

JANUARY 10

Just at dark Katie and Walter arrived home from town after a hard jaunt in a lumber wagon. Katie has a new outfit: an astrakhan coat, a pretty dress, a hat, and a valise, which fits her out for a visit in Wisconsin where she expects to meet all the family except Walter and me. Whatever will I do without her!

I have written to Daniel and Nellie for it doesn't tire my eyes so much to write as to read. I feel very badly to have my eyesight failing, for if I could not read I should be miserable indeed.

Walter got four volumes of *Universal Knowledge*, an American addition to his *Encyclopedias*. He also brought another book, *The Gray Woman* by Mrs. Gaskell.

JANUARY 15

Harry took Katie to Fargo last night and she is on her way by now.[1] How I hated to have her go! But if I had told her she would not have gone. I could not sleep last night. Katie always sleeps with me and I was alone in the lower part of the house. I had tooth-ache again, a sort of neuralgia all over my head,

---

[1] When Katie reached Kingston, she found in her valise a slip of paper on which was written, in her mother's handwriting, the following:
Why tarriest thou, dear Katie?
Lo! in the stormy west
The slain sweet day, with crimson blood
Has dyed the night's dark breast;
And one by one the pale, sad stars
Flare in the distant dome,
And keep a weary watch for you,
Come home, dear love, come home!

and I became very nervous and got up to see if it were morning just as the clock struck three.

The temperature has been below zero all day with such a violent wind that we cannot tell whether or not there is a storm. The snow goes by, not hurrying, scurrying, but whizzing, and never seems to alight. I wished last night, when the wind was shrieking round the house, that Katie's little head lay on the other pillow where it has lain ever since her father died, but I could not be selfish enough to have her stay just to keep me company. I have Walter left to comfort me. He will miss her as much as I, for they spent their evenings talking of their books and solving puzzles, enigmas, and problems; and now he has nobody but me. The puzzle craze seems to have struck the country, for Walter says one sees dozens of them scattered around the counters of stores and hotels in town.

I saw a flock of little, shining birds today, the first ones of the winter. When the snow becomes deeper they come around the buildings more; but there is plenty for them to eat in the fields as yet. Tonight Walter and I saw two Jack rabbits out by the granary door eating wheat. They looked whiter than snow in the moonlight. I went out and got nearly up to them. I wanted to see them run.

Ten degrees above zero; the first time in ten days that it has been so warm. We had a call from Elsie Lessing. She drove down on a sled, and brought the three babies who broke the monotony—as well as some other things. Walter is reading a new book, *Forbidden Fruit* by Hecklander, one of the *Cobweb Series*. He had one of that series before, *Little Good-for-Nothing*.

The storm increased all day until suddenly, at night, it became so still and silent that I was almost afraid. I cannot keep my thoughts from home, now that the children are there. We used to gather in the old brown house on nights such as this, and have jolly times together.

JANUARY 27

Walter went to Fargo to pay his taxes. He could not get into the office until nearly night; so it was totally dark before he reached home, and I was thoroughly frightened. The snow flew with such density that I could see nothing, and I feared he would be lost on the prairie. He said there was no danger, but I was extremely glad when he came in sight. He brought the papers and a letter from Katie which I have read over and over. Everybody travels by sleigh now; and last winter there was no sleighing at all.

I see by the papers that people are freezing to death in the South as well as in Dakota. But I do not think people anywhere else guard against cold as they do here. I doubt if they wear three pairs of drawers, a buffalo coat over a cloth coat, a fur cap, a mask, and arctics over two or three pairs of socks and a pair of shoes. That is the way they are dressed here when they are exposed to storms. Yet some perish in blizzards, though I myself have never seen it.

FEBRUARY 2

The mercury has not shown above twenty below zero, and a blizzard is raging. The air and sky, as far as one can see, are filled with snow driving at a fearful rate. Just at noon, however, the sun shone brightly for a few minutes so that if the ground hog came out he certainly saw his shadow. Gramp used to say, "Candlemas Day, half your corn and half your hay," but that rule will not apply in Dakota. The work has been rather hard on Walter. Jake can't milk, or thinks he can't, which is just as well for him.

FEBRUARY 6

A beautiful morning, enough to redeem Dakota for her last mad prank. The wind has blown the snow into what I call windrows, and covered them with soil so that they look like

118

mounds of earth instead of snow drifts. There are dark clouds hanging low on the horizon tonight, just like March.

I ran out to the sleigh this morning when Walter started for town. I stepped on some ice that was covered with new snow, and before I knew it, my feet went out from under me. I thought at the time I was not hurt, but my back has ached all day. I feel the effects of a fall more than I used to. Walter has made me a plant stand so that I can haul the plants out into the room these cold nights without handling each pot. He is finishing a pair of buffalo horns and reading *The Wandering Jew*, alternately.

FEBRUARY 18

Cousin Daniel has made arrangements for Katie to visit him in Albany. She is now on her way there, going away from her mother just as rapidly as steam can carry her. I hope and pray she will have good luck on her journey. I know she will be safe with Daniel —no better person in this world.

FEBRUARY 22

Raining! Now, will anyone tell me how that can be? Rain, snow, and sleet—first one, then the other! The clouds hang round the horizon, black and ominous. The wind has made the house creak for the last three hours; however, it has finally changed to north, and the storm will probably freeze to death before morning.

Walter got home from Fargo about four, and to my great surprise brought a letter from Katie from Albany—one from Nellie dated the seventeenth, and one from Katie dated the eighteenth. Katie went from Chicago to Albany, a distance of nine hundred miles, in twenty-one and a half hours. The Limited Express is the fastest in the world.

FEBRUARY 27

Sullivan's beer sleigh went by today. If the men get out of beer they go in any weather. Sullivan keeps a hotel at Durbin, eight miles away, and brings his beer from Fargo. I should think he would soon be carrying biers the other way. One is sure to fetch the other in time.

I took everything movable out to air, and put my clothes on the reel to finish drying. I had just gotten them out when I noticed, in the west, a black cloud edged with a light, fleecy border. Suddenly a breeze sprang up. I ran to take in the clothes for the reel was flying around like lightning. It soon began to storm, and in an hour more a regular blizzard had developed. No one would have hesitated to start out this morning; and now I cannot see four rods away. I presume many people went to town, but I hope they will not be foolish enough to start for home.

The stubble is covered with beautiful birds picking up what seeds they can find. I have never heard these birds sing; so I do not believe they are chickadees, although they look like them. It seems warm and springlike to see the chickens around the door. Six of the old hens have died since we shut them up. To be confined seems to be against their nature. Mr. Sampson drove over and brought us four dozen newly-laid eggs. I thought it strange that his hens should lay and not ours, so Walter said he would watch them. He soon saw a hen on a nest, waited until she came off, and saw her eat her egg. I suppose they have eaten all they have produced. We shall have to let them out to break them of it.

The horses are looking well. They are all out prancing about. It is difficult for Walter and Jake to keep them from McAuliffe's. They leave their own stacks and go straight to his. Jack is very useful for he can single out old Buckskin from the McAuliffe horses and bring him home. We have let them out only a few times this winter, for it has been very slippery and they are not shod. The last of our kittens, out of a litter of seven, died last night. They all had fits.

MARCH 7

Walter helped me wash the granary ticks, pounding them in a barrel and running them through the wringer. They look nice and clean. Katie is happy in Albany. She has a dressmaker in the house fitting a new black silk. Apparently her Dakota wardrobe was hardly equal to the occasion. One does not need nice dresses here where there is seldom a chance to go to church. Harry Green came over. Somehow, we do not see him very often now that Katie is away. They have a visitor, a relative of his mother's from Sheffield, England. Harry says the Englishman said they sent all their liars over here to edit papers. I told Harry that perhaps the statement was true, but that all the liars did not become editors.

I have just read this in the *Argus* headed "Blizzard Lie," "Varieties of the Western Roarback—for the East. Our own Northwest blizzard lie. Storm extends from Butte City, Montana, to Chicago; raging with unprecedented fury. Snow one hundred feet deep; stock on western ranges all dead. There will be no more immigration to Dakota. Railroads

122

will take up all tracks west of Chicago in the spring. Everybody, including the oldest inhabitant, dead, the news being brought by a traveling man who was the only person who escaped. Wind tearing up great crusts of earth, terrible, horrible, terrific, awe-inspiring in its strength. The wind cuts like a knife. Terrific roaring; grim death hovers over all the land. Convicts in the prisons all frozen in their cells. Order early. This is gang-sawed, twelve dollars per dozen. Will send screwdrivers to put it on with."

Estelline, Dakota, Bell.[1]

### MARCH 17

The water is running in the sloughs like a swiftly running river, the waves going with the wind. Large flocks of wild geese are flying over the prairies. Walter and Fred went out with their guns, but they could not get a shot at one. The birds are very wild. Walter wants a Winchester rifle with which he feels he could be more successful.

### MARCH 26

There is a blizzard of dust today. The wind has blown a hurricane, great clouds of dust

---

[1] The *Bell*, published in Estelline, in what subsequently became South Dakota, was quite a famous newspaper of its day. Its editor, Hadyn Carruth, was later on the editorial staff of the *Woman's Home Companion*.

flying through the air and sweeping across the prairies. The fine black soil dries on top of the snow as fast as it thaws. Then the dust flies. Part of the time we cannot see McAuliffe's house, less than a quarter of a mile away. The snow has frozen on top just enough so that the horses would break through, which makes hauling difficult.

The boys have been drawing and piling the wood which came to the sidetrack. The carload contained nine cords, and cost $49.50. We burn more wood in summer than in winter, for in the busy season we have a fire in the cook stove from five in the morning to nine at night. The wood is beautiful: straight, dry, and lively. I feel very proud of it. There is nothing more handsome than a nice wood pile. My husband always kept one. When the boys finally finished their work and came in, they were as black as negroes, their eyes looking strikingly white.

Elsie and Lena Lessing walked down to make a call. They think it a short walk, three miles. I have made two crazy blocks which just suit my addled brain. My writing resembles feather-stitching and French knots.

APRIL 10

Seeding is in full swing, and the country begins to teem with activity. The boys have seeded 400 acres this week, walking 110 miles after their seeders, driving their teams. They are footsore and weary after their long tramp. The ground has never been so dry in seedtime since we have been here. In two former springs the men waded in mud and water with rubber boots on. Now dust fills their faces, and they work sometimes in a terrible gale of dirt. I have been out around the fields, but nothing has as yet come out of the ground. Not even a spear of green grass could I find.

Just between daylight and dark, Walter was out working at the cistern when he saw some wild geese fly over and swoop down towards the slough. He ran in, seized his gun, and shot two splendid ones. Now we will have a feast. He brought in one lonesome little buttercup.

APRIL 14

This is the worst day I have ever seen in Dakota. The wind blows without cessation, and the dust flies in great clouds. The boys went out about noon, but could not endure it and came in, their eyes nearly put out. The house is filled with black dust, tight though it be; window sills piled with it. I swept up a dustpan full, upstairs. Dust is even in the closets where there are no windows. Our faces are black in the house.

I am still cleaning the black dust out of the house that blew in Wednesday. But I should not complain for the same day there was a terrible cyclone in Minnesota which tore the villages of St. Cloud and Sauk Rapids all to pieces, killing about a hundred persons and injuring about two hundred more. At least, so it was reported in the papers. The storm struck a house in which a wedding was taking place, killing the groom and nine of the party of friends present, and injuring eighteen others. There has never been a cyclone so far north before, although there have been tornadoes. If the hand of divine providence directs all things on this earth, I hope we shall be directed what course to pursue to escape.

APRIL 24
We have had no milk all this seeding except a quart a day for coffee, which has been rather unpleasant. There are no hills in Dakota, else I should try the old dodge on the cow. We bought two little pigs at Sampson's, and the boys built a small pen for them. The Sampsons said they were going to kill the mother pig to eat *as soon as she got well.*

Yesterday was very warm, and last night the rain began and continued all night. The yard is simply afloat, and at last the dry earth is well watered. Walter says it was the heaviest rain since we have been here. I can see the green wheat on the farther side of the section where the first seeding was done, so the rain was a great blessing. The children go by, barefoot, to school. The rainstorm wound up with a little snow, and tonight the puddles are sealed over with ice.

MAY 1

The wheat begins to look velvety and green. Walter and Mel and Fred went to the Sheyenne and dug some trees: box elders and alders. The *Cyclopedia* says that box elders are ash-leaved maples. The boys set the trees which look very neat right now. There has already alighted on one a little brown bird which sings a melodious song as if in thankfulness. We should have set trees four years ago.

MAY 4

The sun rose in great splendor as it does nowhere else except on these prairies. If any living thing had dared to appear above ground it got chilled last night. The men were off early leaving me alone for the day. I ran to the barn every time I heard a hen cackle; talked to Jack, who they left with me; visited with Roxy; and managed to get through a lonely day, although a long one. Walter has made a hotbed out of two storm windows where we will try to force a few early cucumber, tomato, and cabbage plants.

The elevator hen has hatched twelve chickens which I hope to raise to make up for the brood I lost in the storm last summer. The bottom fell out of a box today in which another hen was setting, and all the eggs crashed to the floor. They were nearly ready to hatch. I have had my plans fall through before, but I was never madder for I had counted my chickens before they were hatched! The boys finished hauling, and the mountain of fertilizer, substance of four years' growth, is spread over the land.

MAY 11

Last night was a warm, moonlight one, and Walter came about eleven bringing Katie, Nellie, and the children.[1] Hattie and Mortie have become great children in every respect. I love them both very dearly. Hattie looks like her mother, but somehow I love her better. She is very womanly. They have been racing around the yard, making gardens and grave yards and enjoying themselves.

There was a fine mirage this morning. I called Nellie from her bed to see Davenport

---

[1] Mortie and Hattie were Theron's children aged six and eight, respectively. They had been left motherless, and Nellie had taken them to bring up.

which is visible only in a mirage. Harry came and took Nellie and Katie to see the farm of Oliver Dalrymple which is near here. He is the bonanza farm king of this region, and his 28,000 acre farm is the largest cultivated area under one control in the territory. His crop has been known to exceed 600,000 bushels; and as many as 195 reapers are used to wake the echoes there in harvest. That ought to give eastern people an idea of the scale on which farming is conducted in Dakota Territory. They went from the Dalrymple farm to Casselton where they ate supper; then drove home in the evening.

MAY 30

Today is Decoration Day and at home there will be a long procession going to the graveyard. The northern people have followed this custom which was started by the women of the south before the end of the Civil War. It is said that the last soldier was discharged from the service on May 30.

> All scattered o'er the southern plain,
> Where shell and bullets fell like rain
> Our dead are bivouac'd. Angels keep
> Their watch above the braves who sleep.

JUNE 1

Tige, our horse, died this morning. Walter, and in fact all the family, felt very badly. We

129

had done all we could for him. It was a sad sight to see him hauled off, so large and handsome and seemingly in good condition. In the four years we have been here we have lost four horses which is very discouraging, and, taken with the low price of wheat, very unprofitable. The white hen came off with only two chickens, so I do not see that I am making a very successful start in poultry. With the dead horse, a dead calf, and wheat at sixty cents the prospect is not very flattering. I fear I shall have to give up stock raising.

The children are always happy. They are out around the prairie all day with Roxy who is extremely fond of them. Mortie looks better than he did when he came. Hattie has a new dress and a new pair of slippers, gifts from her Uncle Walter. Nellie and the children want to leave soon for home, and would like to take me with them; but we have had a visit here, and I should have to part with them soon in any case.

JUNE 10

Nellie and the children concluded to start for home at noon. Walter and Katie went to Fargo with them, where Katie will remain tonight so as to see them off in the morning.

Last night a fearful thunder storm came up with the wind blowing so hard that it shook the house and fairly rocked the granary. I never lie in bed when it storms for I like to see the clouds fly by as they do here in Dakota. They never roll by here. The prairie roses have begun to creep out from the grass. The ground is bright with them and with spider lilies, purple, pink, and white. The daisies have begun to bloom abundantly, great yellow-petaled ones with scarlet centers, and there are plenty of the fine white flowers with a fragrance like lilacs.

### JUNE 16

About noon Daniel arrived at the farm. He has decided to build a new kitchen with a bedroom over it which we need very much, not having sleeping rooms enough. The boys have already begun tearing down my wood shed, dud room, milk house, and meat room, combined, to make room for it.

The boys have been busy pulling mustard of which we have not nearly so much as our neighbors. It is overrunning the country. The authorities are trying to compel the owners of the land to pull it under the law against noxious weeds. The people have been warned by officers of the law that, if allowed to remain, it would be pulled by the county and a tax put on the land to pay the expense. But we think it will be difficult for the county to enforce the law or collect the tax.

Later we went over to the Hayes place and gathered flowers, a great basket full. We stopped the horses on the way back to watch the sunset. Nowhere except in Dakota have I seen anything so beautiful. One can see for miles and miles in one long, unbroken stretch. The prairies are dotted with farm houses, the windows gleaming in the setting sun. I sometimes long for my trees and hills at home, yet nothing can excel this enchanting, endless view. The sun flattens on the prairie until it looks like a sea of fire as it disappears from the horizon.

JUNE 27

My sixtieth birthday. I can scarcely believe that I am nearing the time allotted to mortals. But I am very glad to think that no one would suffer were I to shuffle off this mortal coil.

After supper we all went to the elevator in a lumber wagon. We found some strawberries, and gathered an immense bouquet of lilies, roses, and yellow daisies. It seemed like the days of long ago.

> Forgotten years of silent tears,
> Remembered days of love's sweet praise;
> The long ago of hearts atune
> To glad and happy days of June.

The carpenters commenced the new addition and got the frame up and partly covered

132

the first day (without cider or rum). The new part will go very rapidly. We will have a sitting room, dining room, kitchen, and a good large storeroom or pantry. Now we shall not have to cook in the room in which we eat.

JULY 4, SUNDAY

The glorious Fourth was celebrated yesterday in Mapleton, and the Dodge club went there to play a game of baseball. The boys got home at seven this morning and took the train for Fargo to "see it out." There is a celebration there tomorrow. The boys will return to the farm when their money is all gone —to earn more by the sweat of their brows.

My chickens are all hatched. I have over ninety. We had to make a coop for them as they get so cold out in the heavy dew of the early morning. I gathered a beautiful bouquet without going outside my own dooryard. I never picked a handsomer one in the flower garden at home. A little wild rose has crept into my twelve-foot garden, and this morning it was bright with the loveliest buds and blossoms. No *George the Fourth* or *Maraechal Niel* could surpass it.

> Oh sweet surprise, it seemed to me
> Some fairy hand, my heart to bless,
> Had brought it there from wood or lea,
> It came unsought, 'twas loved no less;
> I stooped and touched it tenderly
> With soft caress.

133

A smoke day like Indian summer, the sun shining without rays all the morning. Two of our Irish boys had a fight yesterday. Tom said Felix called him "onproper" names. They seem friendly today, each minus a good flannel shirt, their faces covered with scratches. They expected to be discharged, but Daniel thought that if they went about their work peaceably he would allow them to remain.

The boys are working on a well and have a curb thirty feet square already down. The rest is to be round, made of narrow boards laid flatways, nailed together, and let down as they go along. It takes five men to work at the well: two that go down; one at the horse; one working the windlass; and one, besides Walter, making curbing. Tom Costello fell into the well today. The rope slipped and let him down twenty feet. He is very strong and quick and, when he felt himself going, he gathered himself for a jump which lightened his fall. He bruised his back and tore the nail from one of his fingers, but he seems to feel quite well.

JULY 22

Cousin Daniel bought a fine span of farm horses, Clydesdales, with beautiful manes and tails. Last week he bought a very neat mare, paying $175 for her. He has made a horsepower to haul up the earth from the well which speeds up the work. They struck gravel today at fifty-two feet. There had been nothing before but stiff blue clay. The quicksand and rocks bother, but water now runs in a very little bit.

Business is brisk on the farm. Walter set the men to hauling the last of the wheat to the cars on the sidetrack. The price goes steadily down. Some of the boys went to Fargo taking ten horses to be shod, and bringing back a new mower, a new harvester, and a new forge. We shall now be able to sharpen our own plowshares. They also brought supplies: a barrel of pork, a tub of butter, fish, coffee, and various other things. Walter made a slop barrel on two seeder wheels which is easily run out onto the open prairie. The ground is too level to pour slops near the door. The boys are playing fire tonight, using the slop barrel for their bucket brigade. Evidently some of them have been firemen.

AUGUST 1, SUNDAY

A heavy dew this morning which rose up and made a beautiful halo around the sun. We hear of hail all around us, but so far we have escaped, and our grain is nearly ready for the sickle. Harry Green is, as usual, our only caller. I am afraid he is trying to get my

Katie away from me. The boys are off playing baseball and, I fear, becoming demoralized. Walter and Daniel are fixing a broken sickle at the forge which will save them many journeys to town. Daniel can do anything in that line. Back east he has built a machine for the manufacture of horse-shoe nails, patented it, and acquired wealth.

AUGUST 6

A beautiful day. The men are all harvesting. Not even a chore man is left on the place. They have been cutting sixty acres a day with all five harvesters running. Some of the men are shocking, and Walter is tagging after them with the horse and buggy. The reapers are flying all about us, stretching out their long white arms and grasping in the grain. They remind me of sea gulls as they glisten in the sunshine. The shocks which begin to dot the prairie look very beautiful as one passes miles of them standing in neat, straight rows —avenues of wheat-lined fields for miles and miles.

The men are getting nearer the house now. I love to watch them work, the grain falling before the sickles at a rapid rate, and the shockers bobbing along, picking up the bundles. The shocks grow very rapidly in comparison to the old way of gathering a harvest.

# Horses

| Name | Age | Bought | Who of | Wt. | Paid | Worth | |
|------|-----|--------|--------|-----|------|-------|---|
| George | 7 | 1886 | D.D. | 2900 | 350 | 375 | } Colts |
| Frank | 5 | 1886 | | 51 | | | |
| Nell | 9 | 1886 | D.D. | 1300 | 175 | 160 | } Matched Team |
| Tom | 14 n 15 | '82 | Hays | 1300 | — | 140 | |
| Bill | 10 | 82 | D.D. | 2200 | 320 | 275 | } Bishop Team |
| Babe | 10 | | | | | | |
| Bill | 12 | '83 | A.B.M. | 1100 | 160 | 125 | } Team Dominick |
| Dan | 16 z 20 | '82 | D.D. | 1150 | — | 100 | } Drove this summer |
| Ted | 14 n 15 | 82 | Hays | 1200 | — | 120 | } Grey Horse |
| Kate | 14 n 15 | '82 | Hays | 1300 | — | 130 | Black Mare |
| Mule | 8 | 87 | D.D. | 1000 | 126 | 125 | } Bot. with wagon |
| Dolly | 9 | 87 | " | 1100 | — | 125 | & Harness for 250. |
| Charley | 8 | 87 | " | 1300 | 165 | 150 | |
| Jumbo | 12 z 15 | 82 | Hays | 1200 | — | 115 | |
| Dock | " | " | D.D. | 1200 | — | 85 | Blind |
| Pete | 4 z 11 | " | " | 1200 | — | 75 | |
| Kibary | " | " | " | 1150 | — | 50 | |
| Buck | 20 | " | Hays | 1150 | — | 25 | |
| | | | Total | | | 2175 | |

A Dakota Threshing Outfit of the Eighties

Dodge Farm, Dakota Territory

Roxy the Dog

Katie drove a harvester one round which is two miles. One can scarcely imagine how much plainer we can now see across to the railroads that bound the prairies.

About five o'clock we saw a shower coming. The men came flying in from the fields with their horses on the run. The wind blew fearfully and the rain fell in torrents. I expect many shocks were blown down, and the grain was lodged. The men cannot cut a full swathe when the grain becomes heavy and tangled.

We have eighteen men now. Every bed is full, even to the lounge. Everything is fuss and clatter. The crops are splendid all over Cass County. Golden rod and asters are in full bloom, and daisies run the gamut of color in lovely profusion. No one need be deprived of fresh flowers in Dakota.

AUGUST 22

Thirty-nine years ago today I was married. That seems a long time, but although there have been many rough places, the years have passed quickly.

Every person and every horse is at work with might and main to secure the wheat crop from storms. There have been many foggy or drizzly days when it was too wet to work in the fields, and the crew were forced to lie around like fish out of water. There have been eight men along looking for work. Patrick Haines left. He could not stand farm work longer. He was a barber from Philadelphia who had gotten out of money in Fargo. Frank Brady came just after the Fourth, ragged and dirty, with not one cent in his pocket. Now, he has fifty dollars which burns him; so he must strike out for Mapleton where, I fear, he will deposit it in a saloon.

AUGUST 31

The first frost. One week ago today the thermometer stood at 104 degrees. Tom just came upon a big stone in the bottom of the well, at seventy feet. They dislodged it, looped a rope around it, hitched on a stout team, and raised it to the surface. It weighs 800 pounds, as nearly as we could guess. If they had struck it with an auger, their seventy feet would have gone for naught.

SEPTEMBER 7

The well diggers struck a new vein of water today. We cannot tell yet what it will amount to. It does not seem to come in fast enough, although it gurgles and makes a great noise at the bottom of the well.

The men finished threshing and brought the machine back onto this place at dusk. We have 13,540 bushels of wheat and 4,004 bush-cls of oats. If we could get one dollar a bushel for it, there would be quite a profit in this year's work. I am so glad the grain is safely harvested and in our own granaries, dry and hard; none of it one bit damp. Walter is very tired. The men have not rested a single day. They seem to have worked hardest on Sundays; however, I suppose if one is to break the Sabbath, one might as well break it all to pieces.

SEPTEMBER 10

Walter set his straw pile at the Hayes place on fire. The flames ran quickly into the stubble, so that all the men with their plows were needed to keep them under control. The wind had changed suddenly and was blowing very hard.

One day during threshing a spark from the engine set fire to the straw, and the wind and heat were so fierce that the men could not extinguish it. The separator and about two acres of grain burned in spite of the efforts of the whole crew. If the men had not started immediately with teams and plows, we might have lost more grain, and probably the house and barns as well.

SEPTEMBER 12, SUNDAY

A hard frost. We are not at work—at least the men are not—and it really *seems* like Sunday. The boys are strolling about, and visiting the threshing machines in the vicinity where there are several still operating. All of our plows have been running. The boys have dug the potatoes. We had 175 bushels, clean, dry, and handsome. All roots that get a firm hold in the ground do well here. Potatoes grow very large and smooth. We have eaten more vegetables this fall than we ever raised for winter use at home. I have brought in probably several wagon-loads from the garden myself.

SEPTEMBER 20

Cousin Daniel is going home this week, and I cannot bear to think of his leaving us. He has been here three months, and he seems like one of the family as indeed he is. Walter went after lumber to build a blacksmith shop, hog pen, and ice house. If Daniel stayed on the farm all the time, he would cover it with buildings. He is happiest when building something.

The men drew out over a hundred buckets of water from the new well, each bucket holding eight pailfuls. It took until noon to get it out so that John could put in the curbing. Walter says we will have to dig a new well; this one has so much water in it. It cost about nine dollars per foot to build. The well-diggers took out three very large rocks and a huge pile of medium-sized ones. It is over eighty feet deep—deeper than any of our other wells.

I have been out around the fields this afternoon. The asters and golden rod are frostbitten. The words of Whittier's "The Last Walk in Autumn" ran in my mind.

> Along the river's summer walk
> The withered tufts of asters nod;
> And trembles on its arid stalk
> The hoar plume of the goldenrod.

SEPTEMBER 28

Twenty-six at 5 A. M. We moved our cook stove into the dining room today, for it begins to be chilly mornings and evenings. Everybody in Dakota gets into as small a space as possible when winter comes. Walter brought letters from my two good grandchildren. Mortie's was printed, but Hattie's was written very nicely, and she sent some pretty cards. I was pleased with the giver as well as the cards.

Just after dinner Walter saw smoke drifting toward the big hay marsh. He started on the run to the upper end of our section where the boys were plowing, and got them to go with him. Many men with teams and plows went; but there was a strong northwest wind blowing and none of them could get ahead of the fire. Between 600 and 700 tons of hay burned, all of ours among the rest. Stacks that were well plowed around were consumed as rapidly as any of them. We paid $100 for the grass, standing. All of Green's hay burned, and several of our other neighbors lost all of theirs, besides all that belonged to the stock yards. The fire started from a spark from a train on the Northern Pacific. I suppose the railroad company will be responsible for the hay burned. But, of course, it is the hay and not the money that we need and want. We have not enough hay to last through plowing. Walter immediately sent two men to the Hayes place to stack oat-straw for fodder. Hay will be both scarce and dear.

OCTOBER 8

The day is a lovely one, but the air is so smoky with prairie fires that we seem shut in. Today I could see a fire way off east of us. I fear more hay is being burned. It seems strange to be compelled to buy hay on these ever-reaching prairies. Nearly all the farmers around here buy the grass and cut it themselves. It grows only on the marshes.

A fire of immense proportions has been raging out west of us, which has swept fully ten miles of country since morning. The stacks are all gone, and farm buildings and towns are in danger. The citizens plow around the sides of the towns for fire breaks. We saw a fire down toward the Sheyenne at noon. It soon ran into a haystack and, as there were several more stacks there, Walter and his men went down. Several stacks burned, but some hay and one barn were saved. Part of the fire started toward the schoolhouse, and Walter and Fred ran with all speed and were just in time to save the building.

We have three buildings being erected at the same time: shop, pig pen, and ice house. Walter is mason, blacksmith, carpenter, farmer, harness maker, and machinist, as well as man-of-the-house and bookkeeper on this farm. Besides these trades, which he plies regularly, he is occasionally a horse doctor and a painter of machinery and buildings.

OCTOBER 14

Twelve degrees above zero at 5 A. M. I dreaded to get up this morning when the alarm sounded, because of the cold. We have no coal and some of the plants chilled a little. Yesterday was so hot that Cripes gave out on the plow and the boys thought him in a dying condition.

Our new well has forty feet of water in it. We send a load of water to the Hayes farm every morning, and give plenty to our horses here, but the water never seems to lower at all.

OCTOBER 18

Four years ago today we arrived on this farm. It hardly seems possible that we have been here so long. When we came there was not a finished building on the place. The house was not done off in any part of it—it was just a shelter. The boys who had been living here had made use of the one room for everything: eating, sleeping, and cooking. They had never washed up nor swept out. I remember how glad I was when I found the floor! Now we have a house, a horse barn, a cow barn, two large granaries, a machine house, a blacksmith shop, a hog pen, an ice house, and, best of all, a good well with water in it. We have had extra work every summer with carpenters and well diggers; but we are all here and we are well and happy.

Harry took Katie to the theatre in Fargo last night to see *Called Back* played. The night was so dark that they did not come home until this morning. The play was given by the Grismer-Davies Dramatic Company, and was taken from the world-renowned novel by Hugh Conway. It was very well acted. Our boys almost never go, for all the horses work in summer, and in winter it is too cold.

Fred goes about once a year when he stays all night and has a good time. Felix and his aunt, Mrs. Harry O'Niel, came out and stayed to tea. She was the first white woman who settled in Fargo.

OCTOBER 23

Last night there was a hard shower. A book agent called just as it was beginning to rain, so we had to keep him over night. Today is very beautiful. Nobody could ask for better weather in any country for this time of year. The men are hauling straw to use for feed. There is a mountain of it stacked near the fence. They are also plowing with walking plows. Fred's feet are blistered, but that will not prevent him from going to town and spending foolishly the money so earned. I can see no falling leaves which I used to think made the autumn sad, but I feel the same. So much plowing around us in the black earth gives the world a funereal look.

Walter brought me a photograph of my old home in Kingston. The trees nearly hide the old brown house, but it looks so good to me. And oh, how different from the bare, treeless prairie! Nellie and Elmore are standing by the fence looking very natural, though not as close to each other as I have seen them when they were younger. Nothing on earth could have pleased me so well as this picture, even though it made me feel homesick. Walter also brought his new gold watch and his new astrakhan coat which is very handsome. None but a fur coat will keep out the Dakota cold. He and Fred each have a buffalo coat. He has commenced his book buying, bringing home a *Cyclopedia of Poetry* today.

There has been great excitement in Cass County over the election of a sheriff. Part of our men are for Benson and part, for Haggart. I shall be glad when the election is over for the papers teem with the meanness of each candidate. One would think they ought to be hanged instead of elected to a responsible office.

NOVEMBER 9

This morning everything outside was covered with sparkling gems. The roofs glistened in the sun, and every spear of grass and every weed was decked with diamonds sending forth their light in all the colors of the rainbow. Walter went to Griffin's and bought four small pigs which he put in the new pen. Not many pigs have such a nice, clean house. Now we have eight pigs, three of which will soon be killed.

The boys have fenced in a yard for the horses, boards, tight together for a wind break. The fence is so high that we can see nothing except sky, which looks lonesome, but the boys will be much warmer pumping water for the horses this winter; and when a blizzard swoops down upon us, we will not be able to see the fence. The machine shop, blacksmith shop, and ice house nearly close up the north side of the yard; and the new fence closes up the west and northwest sides, so that we are well protected. I call it Andersonville; however, there is no danger of anyone's starving to death within the enclosure.

Tonight the air is clear and the moon shines brightly. All night we hear the whistle and jar of the trains on the several railroads which surround us. Train after train passes the elevator coming from Montana, going east. I can see them very plainly with the spyglass.

NOVEMBER 13

I shall not get up until six any more this fall. I have been getting out of bed at five all summer, and sometimes earlier than that, but now that we have only one man, there is no use getting up and stirring up the animals before daylight. We have washed all the clothes from the granary which are the last from that quarter this year. There was a grand mirage this morning. Katie and I, as we hung out our clothes, watched a train sailing in the air; but we could see none of the farm houses between the cars and us, although there must have been many. We could see timber a hundred miles away; while villages ten miles away looked close at hand.

Cold weather is bearing down upon us and I dread it, for when winter really comes there is not much chance to do anything indoors or out. The boys have been digging out and curbing the well on the Hayes place. Walter came in so covered with mud that I would not let him sit down until he had stripped off his pants. He has brought home the magazines which he was having bound: twelve volumes of *Harper's* and two old *St. Nicholas'*. Very nicely done they are, too. I am knitting Mortie some little red mittens. I wish that I had his fat little hands to try them on, but Nellie said to take pattern after a pumpkin seed.

NOVEMBER 19

Emma Griffin brought us a turkey for Thanksgiving. I almost dread the day. It seems only yesterday that, on just such a day as this, my husband and I went sailing up the pond at home. John took his gun and we landed on the opposite shore and hunted squirrels all the afternoon. It seemed too pleasant to last, and in two short weeks he was gone from me forever. I always feel more lonely at this time of year.

Walter took Roxy to Fargo last week to have her photograph taken by Mr. Logan. He brought home the pictures today. She shivered and they are a little blurred, but they look very good to me.

> Blessings on thee, dog of mine,
> Pretty collars make thee fine
>   Sugared milk make fat thee.
> Pleasures wag on in thy tail,
> Hands of gentle motion fail
>   Nevermore to pat thee!
>   —ELIZABETH BARRETT BROWNING,
>     *To Flush, My Dog.*

NOVEMBER 26

Garvey, the last hired man, left last night, and the Woodward family are alone on the Dodge farm. It is quite a change from eighteen or twenty in the family to four. I wish Theron could visit us now. It is nearly four years since he was here. The day has been a quiet one, and we have all been reading, nearly the whole day long. I have read *Harper's Monthly*, "Easy Chair" and all. Walter takes the Fargo papers and the *Weekly Wisconsin;* I take the *Examiner,* Katie, the *Ladies' Home Journal;* and Fred, my baby, the *Police Gazette.* Fred is reading *Little Dorrit.*

NOVEMBER 30

A snow blizzard. The air has been full of big white flakes, flying from the north and piling up into great drifts. The snow is piled as high as the windows at the cellar barn and at one end of the horse barn, in spite of the fact that the fence is eight feet high all around them. Mr. McAuliffe went to Fargo yesterday. He reports that the road is very bad, and that he froze his nose. Harry came and I would not allow him to return home last night. Walter set off for the elevator at 8 A. M., with the thermometer at thirty-four below. He was out all day yesterday and for five hours today in the intense cold, drawing wood. He had to go without his dinner, but he would never complain. How unlike his mother!

DECEMBER 8

There is more snow than at any time last winter. My house plants look very well, a window full of them, and will remain so all winter unless the coal fire should go out, when they would all go. Green's have already lost all of theirs. Katie and I have done a two weeks' washing, hanging our clothes in the new chamber which is a capital place. Everybody in Dakota should have a covered place in which to hang clothes in winter. It would pay a man as well as anything he could build. It

150

would save the wear and tear on the clothes, besides the health of the ones who hang them out.

Elsie and Lena Lessing are hauling wood with a four-horse team. Elsie stands up on her load and touches up the leaders with her whip like any man. They have done almost all the work on their farm this season: plowing, seeding, and harvesting. I cannot understand how any female can do such work as they do, yet it is plain that they are females.

DECEMBER 11

The boys have commenced sawing and hauling ice on the Sheyenne. Ice is a hard-earned luxury when one has to procure it in such extreme cold. They cut great shining blocks. The road is usually filled up and must be broken, consequently they can haul hardly more than one load a day. There is nothing much for men to do here in winter, and unless they have homes of their own, they leave when fall comes. I think this retards settlement in Dakota.

Fred has spent the last two winters in Wisconsin, but I hope to keep him contented here this year. Walter brought in a very large, handsome fox this morning which had eaten the bait set out for him. Some days we see as many as half a dozen.

We have double windows nearly everywhere. The frost collects on the outer ones in
thin and beautiful designs like flowers in lace
work. It is one of nature's winter beauties.

> They are the ghosts of the flowers,
> The blossoms of fairer hours,
>     I see on the windowpane.
> They died in woodland and heather,
> But lo, in this wintry weather
>     Their petals unfold again.

## DECEMBER 25

Merry Christmas! Walter brought a Christmas box from Nellie containing presents for
all of us. It seemed nice to be remembered.
We have been alone all day, and have eaten our
roast turkey and cranberry sauce. I only hope
there are none worse off than we, but I fear
there are, even in this land of plenty. I have
always wished for money at Christmas time
with which to make many hearts glad. For
he who has it and hugs it tight at this time,
will never see where the Christ child lives in
heaven.

## DECEMBER 28

There is now so much snow, with so few
fences and roads, and such long distances between houses, that many people get lost after
dark on the prairies. One of our neighbors
was lost the other night. He drove to a house

two miles out of his way, on a road which he has traveled for the last eight years.

The snow is piled in drifts so high that the boys could not get to the pig pen today. There has been a perfect whirl of snow between that and the blacksmith shop. One might as well try to shovel in a cyclone. The horses seem to thrive on the straw that the boys feed, out-doors when possible, from an immense rick that forms the north side of the yard. The drifts reach the machine shed windows, hid-ing the elevator from view, and shutting us off completely on the north and northwest. Fortunately our coal is in the back kitchen, or we might have to shovel daily for that.

I have frozen one of my fingers. I cut it the other day, and went out not longer than five minutes, forgetting there was a rag on it, and when I came in, the end, as far down as the string, was frozen—rag, finger, and all. The boys have frosty mustachios. They have quite a task to keep the icicles from them.

DECEMBER 31

The sun came up this morning with two dogs which were so bright that we could scarcely tell, except for the position, which was the real sun. They have followed the sun all day and are setting tonight with the same bril-liancy. Fred says it should be an enlightened country where they run three suns. They may be a sign of cold weather, but if it becomes any colder, heaven help us!

The year is about to close, and with it, my ill-kept diary with its blots, mistakes, joys, and sorrows. It seems like taking leave of some old friend. It has offered me much comfort, and helped me pass many leisure moments. I have enjoyed putting down many a pleasant little verse or remembrance which has fitted the day and expressed my thoughts better than I could myself.

> 'Tis midnight now, the year has gone,
> Gone, gone with all its woes and sins.
> God help us through the uncertain one,
> The year that now begins.

1887

The grain pours down in golden treasure,
With flow unchecked and rounded measure,
And through Duluth from this Fargo
It rushes on to Buffalo.

# 1887

THE fifth new year finds Walter, Katie, Fred, and myself still here, and still the same only so many years older. We are well, and although we are sometimes lonesome, we are not unhappy. It was forty-two below this morning at eight. We are completely banked in on three sides with snow. The boys are busy a good share of the time taking care of the sixteen horses, the cow (that gives milk), the fifty hens, and the six hogs; besides bringing in the wood and coal for the stove. Poor old Roxy cries when she goes out, and limps when she comes in. A dog likes a pat on the head no less because she is old.

Walter is making out his quarterly report. He says the new well cost only $260. The others have all cost more. As he has done for the past three years, he has again presented me with a handsome diary which deserves better treatment than it will receive at my hands. He exchanges with me for the old one.

> I closed a closely written book last week,
> A volume which no eye but mine will seek,
>   Among the folios laid away.
> If on each page I did imprint fair flowers
> Of deeds, or naught but wasted hours,
>   No one save God and I can say.

157

Forty-two below at 8 A. M. which is as low as our mercury will go. Forty-eight at the signal service.[1] My frozen finger bothers me. It is peeling and stiff and cold, but all I have to do at present is to feed a small family. Walter went to Fargo as our groceries were getting short. I was afraid he would freeze, for the wind was blowing, and any Dakotan knows what that means in winter. He wore two fur coats, one astrakhan and one buffalo, besides his under coat. The last hour that he was out was a hard one for me. I thought surely he would get lost and perish, but he arrived safely home at last with a good bag of mail. The *Daily Sun*, printed in Fargo, and *Scribner's Monthly* kept us from getting lonely tonight.

JANUARY 14

Yesterday was the first day that the thermometer has registered above zero, and we were all elated. I began washing, and even the chickens came out and crowed in glee. Last night after I went to bed a Jack rabbit came and looked in at my house plants. Katie said he looked beautiful. No doubt poor bunny was hungry and wanted to eat his granny's

---

[1] Forty-eight degrees below zero on January 8, 1887, was the lowest temperature ever recorded by Mr. R. J. McClurg, meteorologist at the United States Government Weather Bureau at Moorhead, Minnesota.

plants. I have a cluster of fuchsias just opening, and how exquisite they look to us here, in this wintry gloom.

> More precious than a garden full of flowers
>   That bloom in summer's prime,
> Are these, that grace the heavy-winged hours,
>   Of barren wintertime

This is the coldest blizzard since we have been in Dakota. It came on so suddenly that I am afraid someone has perished. The snow has been going by for days. The drifts are immense all around the outside of the buildings and enclosures. The snow is a foot higher than the eaves of the machine house. If it keeps on heaping two months longer, I do not know where it will end. One more storm and we shall have to tunnel everywhere. The boys shovel their way around now to do chores. Fred shovels out the pump every time he gets a supply of water for the house. He has been shoveling snow off the roof of the tool house, sliding down on his scoop shovel, calling it his toboggan.

> All day the gusty north-wind bore
> The loosening drift its breath before;
> Low circling round its southern zone,
> The sun through dazzling snow-mist shone.
> —WHITTIER, *Snow-Bound.*

Walter brought me another pair of woolen shoes, without which I could not get along here; also a Dutch calico gown and a felt petticoat, both very handsome. If I just say I want anything, it is forthcoming the first time he goes to Fargo. He bought *Les Miserables* and has already been reading it. We have one sleigh, which has been of no use the past two winters; but this year our wagons are useless. Harry lost his way after leaving here last night, and turned back. He is often snowed in here for two days at a time. I worry so much when our folks are away. Walter has never failed to get here somehow. He seems to delight in hardship.

This is indeed a hard winter. People say it is the hardest one for seven years, though Walter thinks all winters might be as bad when there was such a quantity of snow and no thaw to lay it. The weather is so extremely cold to have all this snow to shovel. We have sixteen horses, but they cannot shovel snow. I think we should have a snowplow. The drifts reach the gable-end of some of the buildings. Fred goes down completely out of sight, where he has a hole in a drift, to pump water for the house. He has a regular tunnel into the cellar house which he shovels out every time he goes after vegetables.

The papers are reporting cases of people and cattle freezing to death. A Fargo girl who went to her claim in Dickey County froze to death there alone. A farmer living two miles north of Mapleton went to Fargo on the train. He came home at eight in the evening, and started to walk from the station in a blizzard. He lost his way, and was found in the morning frozen nearly to death within half a mile of his home. He had on a buffalo coat which probably saved his life; but his hands and feet were so badly frozen that they will have to be amputated.

FEBRUARY 13

The wind blew furiously all night, the snow whirling continually through the air. We suffered with the cold in our bedroom. The snow pelted the windows and the wind came in at every crevice. Katie and I could not sleep nor keep warm though the hot coal stove was close by the door. It seemed to have no effect whatever on the cold. The boys were cold all night the same as we. God pity the people who live in poor houses! I do not see how they live unless God *does* temper the wind to the shorn lamb—but I would not risk it in Dakota. If it would thaw enough to make a crust, the snow blizzard would stop. I never saw a horizontal snow storm until I came here. The snow goes straight by until it meets something to impede its progress, when it flies up in a fury. There is no use trying to live here unless the blizzard is combated with trees, and that will take a long time.

I am so hoarse that I can scarcely speak aloud, which makes it bad for me but good for the rest of the family. I seem to have a cold although I wear a great many clothes, as we all do. I get breakfast in hood, shawl, and mittens as I have done other cold winters. The kitchen is not warm until noon. Every one of us has a cough even to Jake, the Norski. It is night and the blizzard is still howling. Nothing can be seen anywhere except overhead where the moon and stars shine brightly as the sun often does in a blizzard.

> The wintry wind extends his blast,
> And hail and rain does blaw;
> Or the stormy north sends driving forth
> The blinding sleet and snaw.
>> *Winter—A Dirge.*

Burns wrote that a hundred years ago.

FEBRUARY 19

Our horse, Pete, got out this morning and thought, I suppose, to view the surrounding country as Fred found him on top of the drift which runs onto the tool house. His feet were on the bare roof and he seemed afraid to come down. Fred tried to lead him, but he would not stir until the boys had turned him around and given him a few vigorous whacks. We were afraid he would break through and go down at the edge of the roof and be buried in snow. But he came safely off alone at last.

The drifts are as hard as ice. We cut steps in those we pass over on the way to the well and outbuildings. I climbed to the top of the drift which runs to the eaves of the granary, and went all around the buildings. The boys are trying to get an immense snowdrift out of the horse yard, so that the horses will not climb the stack. It is like digging ice, and they get into a great perspiration doing it.

I read in one of the papers that sixty frozen corpses have been found in this country this winter. One poor school-teacher, on her way home from school, was lost in a blizzard. Mr. Reily, who was frozen near Mapleton, died in Fargo. Walter will be lost, too, he is so determined to go when he gets ready. When he comes into view in one of these storms, the horses seem to be flying through the air, there being no background nor foreground—just a shape in the storm. The Lessing girls stopped here today. They have been hauling straw and shoveling snow like men.

It is shovel, shovel, shovel snow,
Shovel everywhere you go,
Shovel high and shovel low,
Shovel, shovel, shovel snow.

### FEBRUARY 27

The storm went down in the night after a forty-eight hour run. The drifts are immense and the farm roads and railroads are all blockaded this morning. The boys get around some on snowshoes. It is a hard task to open the railroads. Walter has seen a train with nine engines bucking through the snowdrifts. The companies hire every man they can get to shovel snow along the rails.

This is the first day that it has really thawed. The eaves run, and tonight is warm and pleasant and the moon shines, bringing peace and cheer to us tempest-tossed Dakotans. We have had a three-weeks' pull with colds. Mine nearly wore me out. I could not get up one morning. Katie and I are very thin. We have had no appetites and there has been little to laugh at in Dakota this winter. It has stormed three months, and we are weary and need a rest.

### MARCH 1

With rushing winds and gloomy skies
The dark and stubborn Winter dies:
Far off, unseen, Spring faintly cries,
Bidding her earliest child arise.
   March!

—BAYARD TAYLOR, *March.*

164

March has come in mild and lovely and not one bit like a roaring lion, although I have no notion it will make a difference with its exit. Almost daily the sky has looked black and threatening, dark clouds have rolled up in the west at night, and the winds have never ceased their hammering. But the last three warm days have settled the snow so that it could not fly. The drifts are black. The dark soil mixes with the snow, and a little thaw leaves all the dirt on the surface.

MARCH 17

A bright spring morning. The drifts are settling into curious shapes like those of the Arctic regions. One big drift hangs from the gable-end of the machine shed which resembles a great white bear. Since the thaw it has a Roman nose. Everything is ice-coated. The south sides of all the buildings have rows upon rows of long, pointed icicles hanging from their roofs like fringe.

Our hens are beginning to lay and we will have plenty of eggs from now on. Our new Poland China has one little pig. Shell sent us a kitten from Fargo, a pretty one which I hope we will be able to raise.

MARCH 23

Just zero at seven. This cold wave will stiffen the back of old winter which was getting weak and spongy. There is nothing in this place to herald the approach of spring. I suppose at home my dooryard is already showing the swelling of buds, and perhaps the tulips are peeping out, but Dakota is bare. There must be hundreds of children in this territory who have never seen an apple blossom, and what is worse, I fear they never will. The absence of such things takes all the poetry out of life.

Up our long river-valleys, for days, have not ceased
The wail and the shriek of the bitter northeast.
We wait for thy coming, sweet wind of the south!
For the touch of thy light wings, the kiss of thy
        mouth.         —WHITTIER, *April.*

## MARCH 31

March pulls out in good shape. It has been a pleasant month although spring advances slowly. The fields are bare but the snowdrifts are not yet gone. Anything that will stop a handful of snow will start a drift, and for this reason people do not plant trees close to their buildings. The trees on the Mapleton road held the snow until June.

Walter brought a girl. We could not think of having seeders come without help in the house. I have been taking brandy and quinine for my cough. I have never before felt myself so weak in the spring. Warm weather will cure me. Katie has a bad cold. It has been two weeks since I went into the kitchen to get breakfast; however, this morning I thought myself the better of the two. Katie waded out to the tool house and weighed herself. She is lighter than at any time since we came to Dakota—102 pounds is her weight this day. I am afraid the spring winds will blow her away.

APRIL 16

I have been hunting for buttercups but found none. The ground has been ice-covered so much that if a crocus or buttercup has lifted its head above the cold earth, it has been frozen. I heard a prairie hen for the first time this spring, and a meadow lark has just been singing sweetly. I saw two robins this morning close by the house. They looked like old friends, but they did not sing and I do not think they like the country. The little tufts of wild prairie grass begin to look green.

Jim Foley was here to dinner. He is going with his teams to Minot to take a job on the new road. There is a great boom there which will follow the railroad. A train loaded with men went up yesterday. The railroad takes men free from St. Paul.

APRIL 24

The boys are seeding in immense clouds of dust which nearly choke them; but still they keep on. They are as black as negroes when they come in with their eyes filled with Dakota soil. I think it will make the men hard just as it does the wheat. The horses came out in good trim on straw and oats, although we bought hay enough to feed during seeding. The Lessing girls are at it in this wind. They have seeded their father's farm for the last three years. The old man does the dragging.

Roxy took her first ride. She is nearly deaf and blind, and when she runs around the yard a little while, she is lame. Poor old doggy! She seems just as sensible as ever. Although she is fourteen years old and useless, I love her well.

> Therefore to this dog will I,
> Tenderly not scornfully,
>   Render praise and favor:
> With my hand upon her head,
> Is my benediction said
>   Therefore and forever.
> —ELIZABETH BARRETT BROWNING,
>     *To Flush, My Dog.*

The farmers hereabouts have been quarreling over the location of the schoolhouse. They run, with all their men, to school meeting to vote their preference. This they cannot keep up forever, so I presume the building will eventually be moved. One was moved near the Sheyenne until it ended in smoke.

### MAY 1

May Day, but as Katie neglected to tell me to wake and call her early, she has not been a-

Snowplow Cutting Drifts on the Northern Pacific Railroad

Fargo, Metropolis of Dakota Territory, in the Eighties

Threshing Crew of the Dodge Farm

Another View of the Dodge Farm

Maying. I do not think she would find even a buttercup, although Walter has seen crocuses at the Hayes place.

Later. I went out on the prairie and *did* find some buttercups, little, yellow, shining things, smelling of spring. The drought last year killed all of my pansies. The fuchsia has blossomed all winter and is nearly as tall as the window. Walter brought me a cineraria from town; and a young man who once worked here sent me a Chinese primrose.

The hired girl is a regular "hired," and I have to follow her around to cover up jars, tubs, and barrels. She seems to want the bottom piece in the pork barrel. But she is big and strong and knows how to work. She weighs 170 pounds; Katie, 102; I, 116.

The wheat on this section begins to show. The face of the whole country puts on such a change at this time, from a hopeless, dismal black to a lively green. The land in this vicinity is nearly all plowed except in the low, marshy hayfields. Everybody on the Dodge is at work with might and main: dragging, seeding, washing, scrubbing, and baking. Besides, Walter and John are beginning the new fence, the first that has been built on the farm. Fenced grazing land will be much better for the cows than picketing. We have forty acres of good grass land north of the house, not broken, which is excellent pasture. Walter, the mason, built a brick chimney at the granary where the boys sleep, which will be safer when there is a fire there. We have cleaned and washed the pantry, and have taken up Katie's bedroom carpet—the beginning of housecleaning.

MAY 7

The wind blew hard this morning increasing to a gale until, by noon, there was a dust blizzard in full blast. The dust blew in at every crack. If a door were opened it came in, in great clouds. We could not see our neighbors' houses. We clean as fast as possible, but the wind blows the dirt in faster than we can clean it out. This is a hard country in which to keep clean. My plants had to be taken out and washed, the pillows were black, and we had to throw away the milk.

The wheat will soon cover the ground and hold the dirt until people commence plowing summer fallows. The wind keeps up an incessant howling of which we get very tired. The boys have moved out to their summer quarters in the granary. They like it out there where they can spit and smoke and yell.

MAY 13

The wheat fields are now green and bright. I have been up where the boys are peeling and setting posts. It costs only a cent a post to peel them and they last much longer. With two augers in use, the posts are set very rapidly. I seldom go out except to roam around the prairies where I am not afraid to go ever so far, for there is no danger of a man's darting out from behind a tree. If he did, he would be four miles away and I could skip out for home.

MAY 17

Twenty degrees at 5 A. M. Everything froze including one of my house plants. I have been out to examine the hotbed, and found my largest tomato plants frozen black and dead, even though the sash is very close, being made of storm windows. I raised the plants in the house and transplanted them to the hotbed. The cucumbers look pretty white but may revive. I am very much disgusted! I hope the potatoes in the ground did not freeze.

Harry took Katie to Fargo and brought home a new covered buggy, a very handsome one. The weather was unpleasant but the trip did not take them long. They had a good team and they looked as though they were flying as they came across these level prairies. They brought some strawberries for supper, twenty-five cents a box. Katie got her satine gown fitted at the dressmakers.

Today is pleasant with not much wind. It has
tooted a month now, night and day, and the
calm is very welcome. I have been out of
doors all the morning. I fed the chickens,
watered the hotbed, enjoying, above all, just
being out in the cool, clean air.

Katie and Harry went down to the Sheyenne where they say the robins, as well as a
great many other birds, were singing. Birds
do not come out onto the treeless prairie very
much. Walter has been pumping out the cellar. It was up to the potatoes (I mean the
water was). There has been scarcely a Sabbath since we have been here that he has not
worked some part of the day.

MAY 30

A bright morning, the grass glistening with
dew. Last night was so cold that we were
afraid of frost, and Walter stretched a canvas
across my little flower garden. The red peonies are just opening, and they look so homelike and old-fashioned. When I was a child I
sometimes used to be allowed to pick one of
my grandmother's.

There have been several showers. They
come up in the northwest, roll up overhead—
when we get the wind and rain—and pass on
to the southeast. The sun comes out between

showers, and it will often commence to shine before the shower is out of sight. I have seen rain falling hard in four directions while the sun shone here.

Roxy and I are alone this afternoon. She is a great deal of company for me, although she is so old that she would be considered a nuisance by some.

> But oft when burdens press me sore,
> And my poor mind befog,
> No earthly good can sooth me more,
> Than waiting on my dog.

Today I saw a cow feeding in the wheat on the other side of the section. Jack could not see her so far (one mile) in his low position for a little rise in the land. So I took him up onto a hayrack and showed her to him; whereupon he started straight for her and took her out. He drove her to the nearest farm house and left her. He is a very intelligent dog and we all love him.

JUNE 6

We get up every morning at four o'clock. The men take care of their horses and eat breakfast just before setting out. It is a long time until noon to go without food. The new man, Nels Nelson, is quite tony wearing two gold rings, gold scarf pin, and gold neck button. He can read English a little. Jake can't, but he takes a Norwegian paper. Dominic Devanny, whose home is in Kingston, has worked for us every year since we came here.

Walter, Fred, and Nels are working on the road; Jake and Dominic are plowing; Katie is sewing; and it would be impossible to tell what I have been doing but I am tired, nevertheless. This evening Harry, Katie, and Fred are going to a party. It has been two years since they went to one in Dakota.

JUNE 12, SUNDAY

A bright, beautiful day after a nice, still rain which was unlike Dakota. I went out around the prairie and gathered a bouquet of many colors and varieties of flowers. People say the wild flowers are rapidly disappearing from the prairie, as they would, for nearly the whole country is sowed to wheat or mowed for hay. The rose bushes which grow among the trees are very large. On the open prairies they die down winters and come up again beautifully in the fallows. A letter from sister, Isabinda. Dear Isabinda, her heart is in her husband's grave. She has not the nerve to get any enjoyment out of life without him, and she says she only wishes to go to him.

JUNE 17

Harry says that wheat has taken a great fall at Chicago which we hope is not to last. Walter thought that when the price was seventy cents the wheat should be delivered, but he had no orders to sell from Cousin Daniel.

A neighbor, a Swedish woman, came to wash the granary bedding. She could speak very little English, so Fred said I was to shout at the top of my voice in broken English. Elsie and Lena Lessing have been hauling wheat to Fargo. They come rattling by with no seat in the wagon.

JUNE 19, SUNDAY

The roses are in bloom all over the yard, peeping out of the grass in a most fascinating way. There is a snow-white blossom which looks like a syringa that makes an attractive bouquet when combined with roses and the lovely grasses. One of these looks like pampas grass only that it is smaller. I cannot go to the garden without gathering a nosegay, for one feels so free to gather, without stint, wild flowers on the prairie where they grow so plentifully without cultivation. My peonies are beautiful with ten blooms on the old-fashioned red one, and twenty on the rose and the white. Walter brought some very handsome daisies, red centers and orange petals. He had pulled them up, roots and all, and set them in the rear of the buggy, and they came nodding into the yard.

A storm came up at noon: wind, rain, thunder and lightning. It blew terribly, great clouds of dust rising from the plowed fields like a cyclone. Later. We heard that this was a cyclone at Grand Forks.

JUNE 21

The wind blows all the time, not gentle zephyrs, but a regular hurricane. Sometimes, when it goes down just at sunset, the air is so pleasant as to almost atone for the wind's fury. It is tearing my tomato plants to shreds although we have protected them with shingles and boxes. There is little use trying to raise tomatoes here, for if they mature they are of inferior quality. The leaves and vines are all whipped to tatters, and the vegetables are unearthed. We have potatoes, onions, peas, radishes, beans, beets, and carrots all up. Fred set twenty-five cabbage, forty tomato, and twenty-five cucumber plants. We plant the latter in paper boxes in the hotbed and transplant the boxes to the garden without disturbing the vines at all.

Harry drove round and wanted Katie to go to Fargo with him. Of course she went, although I should think the wind would blow her hundred-pound body out of the carriage. Cousin Daniel arrived at the farm at sundown looking very well.

My birthday. I have lived sixty-one years.
That's about long enough, isn't it? We had
several showers today, well-behaved thunder
showers, which have done an immense amount
of good.

A sad accident just happened. A tiny bird
hung himself to one of our little trees with a
bit of twine he had carried there himself with
which to build a nest. He became tangled in
the twine to a limb, and when Daniel cut him
down he was dead.

Fred's horse, Charlie, was sick all night and
the boys stayed in the machine house with him.
He is a very valuable horse, one of Fred's
span. He fell on his way to Canfield with a
load of wheat, and he seems to have lost the
use of his hind legs. It has been pitiful to
hear him groan. They brought a veterinarian
just at dark who gave poor Charlie some mor-
phine which eased his suffering. Fred, Jake,
and Walter will, each in turn, sleep by him
nights. He doesn't like to be left alone a minute; and when his name is spoken he always
responds in some way, almost humanly.

There was a severe thunder shower last night
about twelve, the moon shining brightly all
through it. I sat up to watch it, remembering

that Annie told Rhoda that no good comes of watching a storm.[1] Yet I always get up to see it through.

Mrs. Dodge sent me a very handsome brown silk handkerchief which Daniel discovered today in his valise. He had forgotten it. I am very glad to see him so well; and it is nice to have him have all the money he wants. I wonder what I should do if I had his means.

> There is a time-worn proverb,
> A wise old saw, I ween,
> Blest be the man who maketh grow
> Two blades of living green
> On arid globe or bleak highway
> Where only one hath been.
>
> —ANONYMOUS.

Walter brought a load of barbed wire which is to be stretched around the pasture. I cannot bear to think of my lovely prairie being enclosed by the ugly-looking stuff.

### JULY 5

The glorious Fourth has come and gone, and the celebrations are over. Fred went from here to Mapleton; took the train to Casselton; went to Fargo on the noon train; went to Moorhead, Minnesota, in the afternoon; then back to Fargo. Thus he passed the day in

---

[1] This refers to the poem, "The Sisters," by Whittier, where Annie says to Rhoda:
Get thee back to the bed so warm,
No good comes from watching a storm.

four towns, one state, and one territory. We could see the fireworks from here plainly enough.

We have ten men, and Katie and I have to work harder than we are able. I might have secured the services of a Norwegian girl, just landed, but I thought if my soul must go, my body might as well go with it. Ella Sampson came to help us. Her mother is anxious to have her learn, and said I was to tell her to "stand up" in the morning. It was 100 degrees at 2 P. M. I thought I must surely give up the ghost while Katie and I were preparing dinner, but a thunder shower at sunset cooled the air, and now it is perfectly beautiful. When Dakota is pleasant it is so very much so!

JULY 11

The new man was left alone in the cellar, digging, when I happened to look out and saw him a mile off, going toward Mapleton. He did not even ask for his wages for the one day. Good enough! Walter shot poor Charlie tonight as Daniel thought he had suffered enough. Jack stayed by him all through, not offering to follow the teams away, and walked around him licking him.

A beautiful evening, the great lovely moon coming up a little past ten, and no wind. The

179

Lessings have just completed a new granary, with the exception of the bins, and they are having a dance tonight. Walter and Katie and Fred have gone. The Greens all went. Two of them are girls, one, a young lady from Fargo. They all galloped by here on horseback—on their way to a granary party! One of them rode a beautiful white pony.

JULY 15

Sequel to Lessing's dance. Yesterday a sheriff from Fargo came here and arrested one of the men for breaking the peace (he had arrested several other boys). The boys were not invited to the dance, but they went to it, and stole a keg of beer which Mr. Lessing had placed out in the grass to keep cool. After drinking the beer, they became noisy, and some of them went in to the dance and made speeches, which, with the loss of the beer, were too much for Lessing to stand. Fred was there with a girl, but was not at all disturbed —unless it was by the loss of the beer. Fred and Walter have been subpoenaed.

Later. All three boys, witnesses and prisoner, returned. Judge Plummer called the suit and swore in Lessing, who became angry at the questioning and swore, in turn, at the lawyers; whereupon the judge dismissed the whole thing—quashed it!

A bright, still, warm day. The wheat is beginning to turn yellow and Dakota will soon have on her golden gown. Katie found some goldenrod which is the earliest I have ever seen. Lena brought me a root of oldman and another of rosemary, and we set them in the little flower garden. Now I think I shall prosper. I remember an old woman who used to bring a sprig of each to church and sniff them as she listened to the Holy Word.

We now have twelve in the family. I bake eight or nine loaves of bread every other day; besides warm biscuits for supper, often, and pies for dinner—pies or puddings. Ella still stays which makes quite a difference in our small chores. Some days I get very tired and have to lie down and rest which I never used to do.

There will come a morning which I shall not see,
And a summer whose sunshine and greenness will be
As fair to all others as this is to me;
But where, when that morning shall dawn, will I be?

JULY 21

Will Duff, the boss carpenter, is here, and the new barn frame is going up rapidly. People think this is a young town there are so many buildings here. I call it Dodgetown. If we kept a saloon it would be a town. That is the first thing in a new western town.

181

Fred and Jerry are in the potatoes. They haul water down in a barrel and put on the Paris green with a watering pot which is slow work on so large a patch. Walter bought a new harvester, and the experts are here to set it up and overhaul the five old ones. There seems to be no end to the hauling of wheat which they take to Canfield, then bring lumber home. They have been at it for over a month now; but if wheat were only a dollar a bushel, I should not care if they hauled all summer.

Walter brought a woman to help us, and it was really high time for Katie and I are tired out. They arrived for supper at which we had eighteen people. Mrs. Doyle is a good, homespun-looking woman, nineteen years old. She and her husband have a farm in the timber of Minnesota. They are very poor so that four dollars a week was some inducement. *Rhea* is in Fargo tonight and Harry took Katie to see the play.

AUGUST 1

There was a terrific thunder storm in the early morning with a few peals that were frightful. I sat up all through it, as I always do, and finally succeeded in getting Fred down from the back bedroom where he sleeps beside a high brick chimney. I think lightning will strike it sometime. The rain damaged the wheat and used up my garden, the wind switching out the vines. Even the cabbages and tomatoes are ruined.

We now have twenty men, all the dining room will hold. We have put a second table at the end of the extension table, leaving just room enough at the ends to get by. We can seat nineteen men and every seat is occupied. We have a good girl this time. She is kind and suits me, even if she cannot do the fancy cooking that some girls have been able to do. The sheets and pillowcases for the twelve beds make big washings. I pound the men's in a barrel so that they need no rubbing. The carpenters usually overlap the harvesters, and I think they will this year, but, thank heaven, we are free from well diggers.

Daniel and Walter went to Fargo where they bought a thresher. Daniel says he cannot afford to hire his threshing done now that wheat brings so little. They also bought twine which is quite an item on this farm; and a horse, a cook stove, and an ice cream freezer. They met an immigrant wagon with one horse and one mule, and Daniel bought the whole outfit.

Mrs. Dodge sent me two lotus blossoms by express. They are great, pale, sweet-smelling yellow blossoms, larger than pond lilies. They grew in Lake Peppin, near St. Paul. I had never seen one before.

Our family has increased until there are thirty-two. We have put a cook stove in the blacksmith shop. The men have taken all the machinery from the machine house and put in tables with bunks overhead, making fine new living quarters. We have a man cook and he has taken sixteen men at his table out there.

The yard is full of threshers. They have been running the new machine to try it, an *Ames* engine and an *Advance* separator. It looks very queer indeed to see an engine running around the yard with no horses attached to it. They whistle and toot and frighten the chickens and some of the horses. At present there is about a mile square completely covered with buildings and machinery.

There is a fiddler among the threshers, and this evening they all went out in the yard to dance. It was a comical sight, ten or fifteen couples cutting around. The hall was spacious and the dancers displayed their muscles and seemed to enjoy themselves immensely.

AUGUST 16

Cold nights are coming and the mornings are chilly too, but the weather is splendid for our business. Mr. Ames, the threshing machine man, came and spent the day starting the new thresher which works very well. It cost $1,-980, but Daniel paid cash and got a little reduction. The place presents a lively appearance now, while there are fifteen teams at work and thirty men besides the family. At night the yard is full of men and horses and wagons; and it is a mighty big yard too. We make up twenty beds and still some of the men sleep in the barn. The men are stacking wheat. They stack right along until the threshers come up to them, for the grain is safe only in the stack. So far they have failed to reach their goal of 1,000 bushels a day.

The new cook says he has cooked in Germany, on ocean steamers, in pineries, and at summer resorts and hotels. He came to us from the Gay Cook House in Fargo. He is fat and lazy and gets mad and scolds us. Daniel bought a cow yesterday, a black one with a white bag. He paid forty dollars for her. She came in two weeks ago. Our one cow, Lily, the snow-white one, did not give enough milk for coffee. They killed our fatted cow, Daisy, today. She weighed 600 pounds.

AUGUST 20

A very hard rain which wet the wheat and stopped the work. The wind does not blow, and the ground steams and will keep the straw wet for some time. The threshers are at play, some at baseball, some at quoits, and the fiddler keeps up the music. The men are digging a well on the Hayes place which will furnish water to thresh with. It is four miles from there to the nearest slough or to the Sheyenne where all the water used for threshing in this vicinity must be obtained. Walter bought a new plow unlike any which we have had, *The Flying Dutchman Gang.*

AUGUST 22

My wedding day. It seems way off in some other stage of existence when I look back at that time. Everything that has happened in my life since I came to Dakota seems to have taken place in another world. There was such a great change about that time. John and Gramp both died, and I left my home and came to a land so different!

> Old pictures, faded long, tonight
> Come out revealed in memory's gleam;
> And years of checkered dark and light,
> Vanish behind me like a dream.
> —PHOEBE CARY, *Old Pictures.*

Mr. Logan, the official photographer of the Northern Pacific Railroad, came and took several views of the place: one of the men all together, two of the threshers and crew, and two of the buildings. There are twelve buildings on the place now, and Daniel will build more in the spring. He has a perfect mania for building.

AUGUST 26

The boys finished threshing and came down into the yard, engine ahead, separator hitched on behind; then thirty men and thirty horses making a long procession which would astonish a farmer down East. The men are all around the place now. Fred is wearing a star, playing policeman. One of the boys was asleep on a bench in the dining room of the tool house when another boy pulled his leg off the bench. The first boy got up and threw a stone which hit the other boy in the breast. Then the fight began. Both came off with bloody faces; and both were promptly discharged by Cousin Daniel.

SEPTEMBER 2

The fields where they plowed are a lovely green, the wheat being almost thick enough for a crop. A thousand bushels of wheat must have gone into the ground on the whole farm. A load of threshers went to Fargo today who, altogether, drew checks for seventy dollars which they will deposit, mostly in saloons. The towns are full of men who have sweated and toiled, and many will leave their money and go out as they came in, with nothing, and winter coming on. One of the boys came back and drew the rest of his money, about eighty dollars, and hurried to town to finish his spree.

The boys finished the fence. There is a neat gate painted white which looks homelike; but somehow I feel shut in since they have put so many fences on the place. I like the broad, open prairie best. We still have it on the east where there is nothing to obstruct the view between the timber on the Sheyenne and us. Walter went to Fargo, where he has not been for ever so long, having had to be at the heels of the harvesters and threshers until he is tired out. He weighs only 127 pounds. He brought the views of the farm which Mr. Logan took. They are very good, the one of the group of men especially so.

Elsie sent me a pumpkin and we are making pies of it. They do not ripen here before frost, nor do squashes, but in our garden where the cook gathered at will for his crew, as well as we at the house, there still remain plenty of vegetables. Our potatoes are smooth and beautiful. We have six acres to dig and get in the cellar before frost. The tomato vines were black before any of the fruit was ripe.

The yard is covered at times with blackbirds lighting right among the hens. Yesterday, a hen hawk swooped down and picked up a large-sized spring rooster. The hawk rose up a little way when Jack saw it and flew to the rescue. It dropped the rooster and Jack jumped high in the air and pursued the hawk a long way. He goes with me to hunt eggs. Today when we went to the barn, he stuck his nose in a hole in the straw and there, sure enough, was a nest of eggs. He is the smartest dog I ever saw, though for fine sensibilities Roxy is as far ahead of him as any female is ahead of a male.

SEPTEMBER 20

The boys are filling the new hay barn with oats, unthreshed, to feed this winter. They have been stowing away the machinery and picking up generally. The harvesters did a pretty clean job of picking up when they left, stealing five new blankets, some tools and other things, the rascals! Dominic plows all the time with a walking plow, twenty miles a day, which I am afraid will hurt him. Walter and Jake are hanging the big new doors on the barn, and John Martin is pumping out the cellar. The water stands in it the year round, but when it comes up as far as the plank floor, they put a pump in the hatchway and pump it out. Walter is striking out land for the plow boys on the quarter section.

If the wind blows east or west,
They can neither play nor rest;
So much work beneath the sky,
They can scarcely stop to die.

The wind has blown a gale all day, and we could not hang up the sheets. I gathered a pile of clean stones which were dug out of the well, and laid them on the edges of each sheet placed on the grass. Without this contrivance they would have traveled across the section in no time. I shall get a patent on it at once. I never knew anything about the force of the wind until I first came to Dakota when, one day, I put a shawl over my head and started for the garden. The wind got inside the shawl and down I went, backward.

SEPTEMBER 24

It has been a beautiful day. I really think Dakota is trying to have an Indian summer as well as she can without falling leaves and scarlet foliage. Katie says there are some lovely autumn colors on the trees near the river. She and Harry went down there yesterday to wander among the trees. They brought home some of the grasses which look like pampas—six feet long, the stalks are, and the feathery silver panicles hanging so gracefully at the tops are beautiful. Walter thinks they might have been sown by the Northern

Pacific Railroad Company who, it is said, has strewn the way with grass seeds of various kinds.

All the men are plowing except John Martin who is choring around the place. He is a good hand at anything. I yell, "Mart!" sometimes twenty times a day, and he always bobs out of somewhere and answers, "yes." He seldom talks in the house, though he has been here every summer since we came, and two winters; but I often hear him sing, and preach, and drum out in the men's room.

OCTOBER 1

From my little bedroom window upstairs, where I now sleep, I can see three electric lights, the two in Fargo and the one in Moorhead. They look as though they were about a rod apart. I can see them without raising my head from the pillow. Walter and Mart are building a small storm house over the front door which will be a little portico in summer when the sides are down. We have had, heretofore, only a double door which could not be opened in winter.

I suppose these are our last warm days and I would so like to be out of doors, but now that we have no girl, I scarcely get time to go to the barn for eggs. Mrs. Sampson came over to help us wash the men's sheets, a dozen of them, and pillowcases, two dozen. She has rubbed all day and Katie has sudsed and rinsed and hung them out. I, for once, have not had a hand in it. I still have rheumatism in my shoulder.

OCTOBER 9

There are fully three hundred head of cattle in sight. The herders have taken them out on the wheat stubble where, if the plowing was done early, there is good pasturage, the fresh green wheat being three or four inches high. There were about a hundred calves on the north end of the farm yesterday. Our own two cows enjoy themselves now that they are not tied up. They each give a pailful of milk. I made eight pounds of butter last week, more than the Dodge farm consumed. There is a large herd of horses on our section which belong to Mr. Garvey who lives down near the Sheyenne. He has a herder, and now that the grain is all threshed, he lets them scour the country unless the farmers dog them off. He has forty western mares, some of them spotted like circus horses, and cattle and sheep in great numbers.

We could not live here, now that there are so many cattle and hogs loose on the prairie, without Jack. He is the best dog I ever knew, just as intelligent as a person, and keeps erything out of the garden. We have seven black cats, but I shall not start to St. Ives for the rats are upon us. The first one was seen on this farm only a day or two ago, but they have been overrunning Fargo for some time. They will be a terrible pest in this wheat-growing country. John just brought in a monster rat from the horse barn. There are no snakes here except a very few large, harmless striped ones. I have seen only three this summer. Roxy has hard work to kill a snake, but she doesn't hesitate to attack one when she sees it.

OCTOBER 15

Harry and Katie came home from Fargo a-flying as they usually do. It frightens me even to look at them, for the horses really appear to be flying through the air. They are a beautiful span, cream-colored with darker, almost invisible spots, and flowing manes and tails. Katie brought a letter from my Nellie.

Our one mule and a horse that mates with him got into a herd a few days ago. Fred and Walter have tried repeatedly to get them home but failed. They were on our section today, and seven of our men on horseback went out to run them in. It was an exciting spectacle. Sometimes the whole herd was galloping at full speed over the prairies for miles

193

and miles, our boys in hot pursuit. They finally ran the horse and mule, with several others, into our yard and secured them.

OCTOBER 20

The gathering of the farm produce has begun. The boys are bringing home 600 bushels of potatoes, which they had dug and left buried in the field until they found that Carney's hogs had started to unearth them. Mr. Carney has 150 hogs, which he has turned loose upon his neighbors, as well as 200 head of cattle and 100 horses—the old scamp! Walter had to take all his men off the plows and set them at the task. They will put part of the potatoes into the old cellar and part in the new barn. We sent a grain-box full (93 bushels) to Fargo for which we received $40. The boys had on four good horses and brought home some wood and five pigs. We are now fixed so that we will buy no more pork on the Dodge farm.

NOVEMBER 3

The cold weather hangs on and the ground freezes deeper and deeper every day. This is a poor country for lazy folks as well as drunkards. Both are liable to freeze to death when the mighty blizzard overtakes them.

Fred and Walter went to Fargo this afternoon. Fred bought a suit of clothes, shirt, collar, cravat, two suits of underwear, box of socks, and still had money left, so he did not come home with Walter but stayed to spend the rest at the theatre. Walter brought me a very nice looking cloak which, of course, doesn't fit; nothing does. Walter will take it back. This is the third one he has brought, all too tight for me. I have not been to Fargo for three years, nor off the farm. I have been home so long that I dread to go anywhere, but I suppose I shall have to go to buy myself a cloak or go without one. I know the children are provoked because I am not like other people.

Walter bought and led home two cows, nice looking animals, only they look too much like oxen to be good milkers. They are dry at present. Today all the cats and kittens came in, seven of them, black and sleek and fat. How they did play! We allow only one to remain in the house.

NOVEMBER 10

Walter brought me another cloak which they say is too large for me. I think it is just right as to size, but it is heavier than I want or need for I cannot go out in the very cold weather that we are now having.

The County of Cass has gone strong for prohibition. Now the saloons will go from Fargo to Moorhead, just across the Red River into Minnesota. I hope the country will soon pass a prohibition law which is the only way to reach one class of drunkards, the man

Who goes drifting along without honor or station,
And gives not a thought to his own reformation.

Walter went to the polls for the first time in the territory to vote the prohibition ticket.

NOVEMBER 19

Last night when Walter came from Canfield, he brought with him a young woman and her baby who had gotten on the wrong train in Fargo and been put off at the elevator. The baby—Dennis O'Niel his name was—was sick and I was up nearly all night doctoring him. He would look at me sorrowfully out of his big baby eyes; but he was very good and scarcely cried at all. The woman had a basket containing some things for the baby, and a very large uncut ruby which she said had belonged to her grandmother. It was extremely beautiful, sparkling with liquid fire in the lamplight. Katie was spellbound and could scarcely take her eyes from it. This morning the baby was better and they have started on their way back to the railroad.

It is snowing today although the sun set last night in a bank of crimson cloud tipped with cold, foretelling pleasant weather. Walter was at work in the blacksmith shop making a door latch when the piece of metal flew from the tongs red-hot with such force as to cut a deep gash in his forehead. He came in all bloody and gave us a serious fright. Had it been Fred coming in at any unusual time of the day, we would have expected him to be hurt.

NOVEMBER 24

Thanksgiving for the sixth time on the Dodge farm. Today I have only Walter and Katie of my own who, with Harry and John, make up our dinner party. We had roast turkey and cranberry sauce and all the other good things. It is storming in earnest and the wind is blowing the snow into drifts. Katie and I are moving the milk and everything else that will freeze into the sitting room closet, for we shall have to shut the kitchen door now after supper to keep the plants from freezing.

NOVEMBER 30

John Martin is going to the woods. I had hoped he would stay, for I hate to have a new man in the winter when they have to sit in the house so much. John has been here four years and so is like one of the family. The boys killed hogs today. Walter has done everything now, sticking hogs being the only thing which he had not tried and accomplished. They killed four that weighed, on the average, two hundred pounds apiece.

I have sewed a little today for the first time in months, with the exception of darning and patching which I do at any and all times. I am making some flannel wrappers. We have to bundle up here in winter until we are uncomfortable, and then shiver half of the time.

DECEMBER 2

Walter returned from town early and I was glad for the snow commenced coming at noon, and we can see nothing now but snow. He looked like a snow man with his buffalo coat driven full of it—perhaps there was a little more expression to his eyes. He brought a letter from Nellie but none from my naughty Freddie. Walter took the potatoes but, as it was snowing very hard, he could not look around for a purchaser, so he received only forty cents a bushel for them. We have the new *Scribner's*, *Harper's Monthly* and *Weekly*, and the *American Agriculturist*.

> The frosty twilight early falls,
> But household fires burn warm and red;
> The cold may creep without the walls,
> And growing things lie stark and dead,
> No matter, so the hearth be bright,
> Where household faces meet at night.
> —ELLEN P. ALLERTON.

## DECEMBER 4, SUNDAY

A blizzard. The snow has fallen all day in a blinding mass, piling into drifts and striking the house with such force that it fairly trembled. How terrible it must be to become lost on the prairie! No road at all is visible and there is nothing to guide a person; moreover it is necessary to get to some shelter before night overtakes one. No one is so well acquainted with the country that he can find his way in a storm such as this. When we look out it is like gazing into an eternal empty space. It gives me a homesick feeling as though I were shut out from everyone except those in the house. I have not seen a team astir since the storm began. The boys can just make it to Fargo and back while daylight lasts if they start early; but they need to watch carefully for it will not do to take risks.

## DECEMBER 10

The wind blew from the southwest last night driving the snow back the other way. Today is quite still. The boys are putting up a snow blockade of wagons, hayracks, and other things to catch the drifts beyond the new barn. The horses still eat at the stack when it does not storm, but there will be many days when they do not go out at all, for horses will not drink in a blizzard.

199

Walter bought a barrel of apples paying $3.40 for them. They will last all winter and make a lot of good living. If we eat all pork and no fruit we will get scaly. John Martin came back with Walter and took up his old position as chore boy. He said he got lonesome. Now I wish Freddie could come in and stay through the evening. I hope to have them all here in the spring.

DECEMBER 14

The little silver birds are here, having come with the first blizzard as they always do. We think they may be driven before the wind. They seek shelter around the stacks and buildings. The boys feed the black kittens at the barn on warm milk. We hope to keep them all, for the rats are numerous and troublesome.

Walter went to Fargo to have Gumbo's tumor on his neck removed by a veterinarian. They could not lead him, so Jake rode him down and back, and Walter went in the sleigh and took Katie. They got some books to send to Nellie and the children for Christmas. They returned just as night was closing in upon us. I was very glad to see them come, as a dense fog had settled down at sunset and it was becoming difficult to find the way. John Griffin came across country in the night fog guided, he said, by the barking of dogs at the farms.

A real blizzard. The wind howls dismally. Nobody who has not seen a Dakota storm could conceive how fiercely they travel across the prairies. To be out in a storm such as there is tonight would be certain death. No neighbor, nor friend, nor physician could be called if a person were dying. I am afraid there are many families who will suffer in this three-days' storm. Not many of our neighbors have coal to burn night and day as we have. I hear there are people who do not undress at all in winter. Roxy went out this morning and was too cold to get back in by herself. Walter heard her cry and brought her in, poor doggie!

I have a primrose in full bloom. How beautiful it looks to Katie and me in this cold, stormy weather! There is also a periwinkle— Chaucer calls it "periwinke"—a modest little flower, snow-white with a pink eye. It looks like a perennial phlox. In the two years I have had it, it has never been without a blossom. I never had a coal fire until I came to Dakota, and I find it rather hard on house plants.

> 'Tis sweet to have when the storms begin
> To roam o'er the earth so wide,
> A little summer all shut in
> From the frozen world outside.

## DECEMBER 25, SUNDAY

Merry Christmas to everybody on this bright Sabbath morning. This is the sixth day of the storm. The presents for the family at home lie here because no one could get to the express office so that the children would receive them in time for Christmas. I hope no children have perished in this storm. There may be improvident families who did not have fuel enough to last six days. If so, God help them!

Mr. Griffin arrived home in his sleigh and brought our mail. I received presents from Mrs. Dodge, Nellie, Hattie, and Mortie; and a letter from Fred which was more welcome than a present, be it ever so costly. I was very much favored on this Christmas day.

## DECEMBER 31, SATURDAY

The boys have been out shoveling. When they came in they were so covered with frost and snow that they could scarcely get thawed out to eat their dinners. Jake is not very rugged, but he can stand the cold better than any man we ever had on the place. I suppose it is because he is a Norwegian. I am writing to Freddie. I miss him very much and find myself continually thinking of home while he is there. I was always watching for him after his father died. He was my baby. He is the life of the house and all the hands like him. I never knew him to have trouble with any of them since we lived on the farm. But he is not strong and tough enough for farm work.

It has stormed all day. If it continues much longer we will be out of coal and that would be much worse than going without our mail. Jake and Mart have no tobacco left, which is serious for them. The wind blows furiously tonight and it is a lonely New Year's Eve. But we are snug and warm and have not got to go out with the day and the week and month and the year at twelve o'clock tonight.

> Poor Old Year, must you go,
> On this cold, stormy night?
> Your garments are thin,
> And your hair grown so white.
> But the New Year stands waiting
> Just outside the door,
> We must usher him in
> And see you no more.
>   So Old Year, goodbye!

1888

How strange it seems,
This changing of dates!
We come within one
Of having four eights.

# 1888

Happy NEW YEAR! The sixth year finds
Walter, Katie, and myself comprising the
family, with Jake and John Martin for help.
It has stormed steadily for two weeks, the
longest storm I have ever known. The snow
flies and the wind drives from the northwest.
The whole country is snow-covered.

Walter thought he must go to Fargo as we
were nearly out of coal and we had not heard
from the outside for a week. It proved a
fairly good day although the roads were badly
drifted in some places. He brought the new
*Harper's* and *Scribner's*, and two *Harper's
Weeklies*, so we are provided with plenty to
read. He presented me with this handsome
diary which he or Katie might keep neatly,
but which is too nice for me to cover with
blots and scrawls.

JANUARY 12

Forty-two below zero. It snows all the time.
The oldest inhabitant has not seen more snow,
but he is not so very old yet, you know. John
G. Whittier's picture appeared in *Harper's
Weekly* last week. If he were here he might
write another *Snow-Bound* but it would

have to be on a different plan. His "tunneled wall" would not stand long before a blizzard. I doubt if there is a poet living who possesses vim enough to write a poem about a Dakota storm. I guess a blizzard would knock all the poetry out of a man. There is no romance about this country. It is just plain business, and No. 1 hard at that.

Katie and I were cold last night in spite of bedclothes and fire. What of the poor children in Dakota homes who do not have these comforts? I could not sleep for thinking of them. Tonight the wind roars and screams around the house. Katie and I have been sitting all the evening with our blanket shawls about our shoulders. Yet I suppose this is the warmest room in Dakota. I know a great many people must suffer tonight.

Poor old Roxy went out and became so cold that she never would have gotten in if I had not gone out and beaten her in. It was some time before she could stand on her feet. Today a Jack rabbit came very near the house. He looked beautiful, as large as a dog and snow white. I beg the boys not to shoot them and then, in summer, they eat my vegetables.

JANUARY 17

Twenty-eight above at last and not much wind. It seems almost like getting left, somehow, to have a decent day. Walter says it will grease up the sleighing. This morning there were two bright sundogs and a rainbow, or snowbow, overhead. I hope the latter has the same significance as the former. I think I should rather be drowned than buried in snow. The frost fell off the upstairs windows in great cakes. Those below, where the frost hangs to the outside ones, are done in arabesques of intricate design: spiked cacti, feathered ferns, and marsh pitcher plants.

These frosty nights against my window-pane,
Nature with busy pencil draws designs
Of ferns and blossoms and fine sprays of pines,
Oak-leaf and acorn and fantastic vines.
            —T. B. ALDRICH, *Frost-Work.*

Tonight the moon shines clear and bright and oh, how lonely it must seem to the friends of the many who perished in the last cold blizzard! Sixty persons are already reported frozen to death and no doubt many on isolated farms not yet heard from have perished.

JANUARY 19

Thirty-eight below and Walter *would* start for Fargo although I begged him to stay at home. I worry all the time he is gone. He wears two fur coats and a mask, but if the horses should refuse to travel or he should lose his way, what then? There are six solitary miles with no stopping places and he is liable to be overtaken anytime by the deadly blizzard.

The papers give accounts of fearful suffering in the last blizzard, the one of the twelfth. Two hundred people are reported dead and they have not all been found. The railroads were blockaded, the snow standing fifteen feet deep in the cuts. The Northern Pacific try to open their tracks by hitching a procession of cars together, headed by a snowplow, and forcing them through the drifts. The boys say they come thundering down the tracks, shrieking and swaying, going at full speed. When they encounter a hard bank of snow and ice, it gives way and great chunks of snow are thrown out over a large area.

There should be no school here in winter. At Aberdeen some children were lost coming from school. The men took long ropes and walked fifteen or twenty abreast, back and forth over the ground. One smart teacher (a lady, of course) tied her scholars together, three abreast, and brought them in safety to a farm house three-quarters of a mile from the schoolhouse. The blizzard commenced about four in the afternoon and scores of children perished all around the country. Many of their poor, little bodies still lie under the drifts.

Many people suffered the loss of their stock. The Fargo *Argus* reports two thousand head of cattle, sheep, and horses lost or frozen to death. People tell of having blizzards east, but nowhere except on the prairies can the wind gather such force. Nobody except those who have heard it rave and tear and shriek and roar, and have seen the snow fly by horizontally, cutting the air with a whistle like bullets, can imagine how fierce blizzards really are.

JANUARY 22

The sun shines very brightly with nothing to rest the eye upon—just one gleam of whiteness. We received a paper from Theron containing an account of a blizzard in Chicago, but there are few in our papers. They seem to suppress everything injurious to the country that would tend to stop immigration which is a fearful thing to do for, while there are not many chances to secure a home on earth, there are some chances to secure a home where there are many mansions, through the deadly blizzard. "In the midst of life, we are in death."

Nellie was feeling anxious about us, but if anybody freezes to death on the Dodge, it will be on the outside. Walter takes every precaution to make us comfortable, and if he doesn't get lost coming from Fargo, we are safe. Tom Carney got lost and lay out all night, but Walter's head is always clear. No whiskey ever possesses his brain.

The storm was indeed very bad all over the territory. At Huron, a Mr. Robert Chambers and his two sons, aged nine and eleven, started to go a mile to water some cattle. The father was on foot and each boy was on a horse. The father sent the older boy home as he was troubled with rheumatism, and then, with the younger boy, tried to drive the cattle home. Johnny lived through and told what happened. The father wrapped the boy in his great coat, made a place in the snow, and called their St. Bernard to him. The boy was warm but knew that his father was getting cold. They talked together through the long, bitter night about perishing. They said a prayer together, and soon after, the father died. Johnny was rescued next morning by a searching party.

JANUARY 24

The wind came up last night and by twelve another blizzard was upon us. This morning I could only now and then see the buildings. Great masses of snow were driven against the windows where they stuck fast. That never happens in a very cold storm. The blizzard finally abated somewhat, and the boys went out and sawed and put in place the two loads of ice which they had gotten in Fargo before the storm. It will fill the ice house and I am very glad. It is two feet thick and clear as crystal, much nicer than the ice from the Sheyenne. Now we will drink Red River water.

Cousin Daniel writes that he is thinking of selling the farm in the spring if a good offer is made. He thinks farming does not pay at the present price of wheat and with no prospect of a rise. He has made so many improvements here, which the average farmer does not take into account and will not pay for, that the place will have to be sold at a great sacrifice. We have been here so long that leaving the farm will seem like again leaving home. Except for the cold winters, I should like this place very much indeed. I like a farm better than a home in town; however, for the rest of my days I do not expect to be considered nor consulted as to where I should rather live. But I'll keep up with the procession as long as I am able.

> I'll swing what way the ship shall swim,
> Or tack about with equal trim;
> Whatever turn the matter takes,
> I'll deem it all but ducks and drakes.

Last night there were six Jack rabbits playing in front of the door. They did not seem at
all afraid even when Jack went out. They
have lived under the granary for a long time
and he has given up chasing them for he
knows he cannot catch them. Last summer,
after they had eaten off all my string beans, I
was almost sorry I had not let the boys shoot
them.

I have been thinking how this lovely day
must affect those who lost fathers, mothers,
sisters, and brothers in the storm which has
swept so many human beings off the face of the
earth. How the mothers' hearts must bleed
whose children went away from home in health
and happiness only to be returned to them
frozen corpses! Miss Ella Lamar, a school-
teacher, and one of her pupils were lost. When
they were found, the kind teacher had the
little girl clasped to her breast in a vain endeavor to save the child from her awful fate.

The newspaper editors were out of paper
and many of them were compelled to print
their regular editions on blue, red, brown, or
any kind of paper which they happened to
have on hand. Some of them ran blizzard
editions with casualty columns.

The biggest authentic blizzard story which
I found in the papers was as follows: Mr.

Eric Johnson went out to water his cattle. Among the drove was a large ox. The cattle, one by one, dropped in the snow from exhaustion; and soon the ox became bewildered and lay down in the snow to die. While the man was floundering around in the snow himself he had an inspiration. Drawing his knife, he killed the ox, disemboweled it, and crawled inside. After drawing the sides of the stomach together, he was perfectly sheltered and was kept alive by the warm carcass. In the morning the hide was frozen completely stiff and he could not get out, but he kept calling for help until someone came to release him.

FEBRUARY 9

The mercury ran down into the ball at midnight and did not come up until 9 A. M. Our folks think it must have been fifty at daybreak. There are three suns sailing the Dakota sky, but they fail to warm up this desolate region. Jake calls the two bright dogs "sun devils." The boys tipped over five times with their first load of straw. They are now at work in the granary cleaning wheat which is a standing job on this farm. They would clean the whole 12,000 bushels if they could and save the elevator charges and the screenings.

Harry came for Katie to make his people a

visit. I consented to let her go but not to come home after nightfall, so she will stay there until morning. Mrs. Griffin and Mary came to spend the evening, and I was very glad for the house seemed lonesome.

FEBRUARY 13

This morning a light, frosty snow which shone like diamonds filled the air, and the whole world appeared to be made of snow. Walter churned for me today: worked, salted, and moulded the butter in fine style. We color it and it looks very neat made into half-pound balls and stamped with a strawberry mould. We got seven pounds of beautiful butter from one week's milk. It is thirty-five cents a pound in Fargo.

The storm started early and has increased all day. We think it fully as bad as the one on January 12, but I hope people are not out in this one. There are great numbers of cattle exposed to blizzards here and they suffer terribly, even to the death. There should be a law to protect them. Ours have a good warm place and the men do nothing except look after the stock, but even so they get frostbitten. One of our cows froze her teats coming out to drink.

Nine o'clock in the evening. The storm still rages and only occasionally are the out buildings visible.

Poor naked wretches, whereso'ere you are,
That hide the pelting of this pitiless storm,
How shall your houseless heads and unfed sides,
Your looped and windowed ragedness, defend you
From seasons such as these?
—SHAKESPEARE, *King Lear*.

FEBRUARY 16

Pleasant again with a grand mirage. The country on a morning like this looks beautiful beyond description. Walter brought Fred. It was fortunate he arrived on such a nice day, for he might have been snowbound in Fargo a week or longer. I was very glad to see him, and we have been talking busily of old Wisconsin friends and places where he visited.

Walter let the hens out around the door. They are of every color and breed, which is what I like to see. The Lessing girls went by, hauling wood to Canfield. Such young, slender German girls, how they can work like men is beyond my comprehension. They drive four-horse teams standing up like any teamster.

Walter starts this evening for Kingston. I hope he may have good luck on his journey, for if anything should happen to him it would harm us all. He is the backbone of the family. There are not many boys like him, at least in my family.

FEBRUARY 28

The air is filled with flying snow which goes by as though it had no intention of falling.

The dirt flies with it, and great lumps of crust go crashing through the air. One would suppose that all the snow in the heavens above and on the earth below was flying at the same time. It comes first from the north, then from the south—never from the west in winter. Saturday's, Sunday's, and Monday's snows are piling up into drifts to the tops of the doors at the barns and granaries. It is well that there are doors on both sides of the buildings for sometimes one side is drifted in, and then the other. Harry came, the wind being at his back, and did not dare start home as the road was lost before he got here. Somehow I do not think he was very anxious to get away.

MARCH 1

March has come in like a lion, a roaring lion at that. I should suppose newcomers to this territory would pull up stakes in the spring, and old settlers would follow suit. It does not pay to endure these hard winters with wheat at fifty cents a bushel. The snow which has fallen the past two days is flying over the prairie in a blinding mass, the sun shining through it. I pray it is the last storm of the kind we will have this year.

The snow is piled against the south sitting room window within one pane of the top. In front of it, inside, is my plant stand with all the beautiful flowers in bloom. The background looks queer and the foreground looks cheering. Fred and John have shoveled all day for the snow has drifted against the stacks and doors and gates.

MARCH 4, SUNDAY

A still, bright, gleaming morning. The ground, snow-covered, glistens with Dakota diamonds sparkling in prismatic splendor. It looks like spring but thaws very little as yet. This has been the hardest winter in our six years in the territory. The drifts are very high and the horses jump out and make us a great deal of trouble. Pete got down into the yard today and rolled onto his back between the drifts and the stack. Mart could not get him up alone, so Katie had to go to McAuliffe's for help.

MARCH 11

I have found fault with Walter because he did not write, and yesterday Fred brought six letters from him dating all the way from February 22 to March 5. I suppose they were delayed by the storm somewhere on the road. This should teach me a lesson in patience, but I am afraid I am too old to learn.

The boys had just let the horses out when the snow began to blow in a fury, apparently filling the whole world. When the wind began to lull, the prairies looked like an ocean lashed by angry waves. It is such a wet storm, sticking all over everything and sounding like hail. The snow sinks lower and lower until it finally crawls over the prairie close to the ground. I do not see how this vast amount of snow can disappear in time for seeding.

> Tomorrow is a day too far
> To trust whate'er the day be;
> We know a little what we are,
> But who knows what he may be?
> —LORD LYTTON.

MARCH 22

Twenty degrees below zero. How is that for spring? Winter can't even get into the lap of spring until some of these immense snowdrifts are out.

Blockading the railways, the lanes, and the byways,
Delaying the mails and obstructing the highways,
If I could be weather clerk an hour or so,
I'd make it right warm for the beautiful snow.

I shall be very glad when Walter returns. I have never been separated from him so long since he was born. I have written him that we are frozen up as yet, with no signs of spring; so he might as well finish his business and his visiting. He has been here six years with only two weeks vacation which he spent in Kingston three years ago. He has never, until now, visited Theron who has been away from home a long time.

The snow is piled mountain high and still it comes. March can be compared to a roaring lion right through this year. It is almost four months since our first blizzard. What a prospect for spring! I am sure there will be a flood. The boys brought a load of coal, for we must keep our coal stove running even though it should be spring.

Walter arrived this morning and I was very glad to see him. He brought Katie a handsome gold watch which pleased her very much. He has visited all his old sweethearts after giving them a six years rest. But still they remain single. His trunk came from Kingston. It is one I brought from Vermont when he was a baby. One of my beaux made it for me before I ever saw my husband. It had a newspaper spread on the bottom which I put there long before the War of the Rebellion. On the whole, I think it may safely be called an *old* trunk.

April fool! Never did I see such an April day as this! The drifts still reach the eaves of some of the buildings; and there has been no water running yet. When I stand in the east

221

kitchen door, I cannot see over the tops of the drifts that have piled up there, leaving just a walk beside the door.

I am nearly sick. I seem to be out of tune in too many places to patch up. Everything ails me. As old Granny Dingman used to say, I enjoy very poor health. Walter brought Mary, an Irish girl who he had engaged in Fargo. She immediately cut her thumb with the chopping knife.

APRIL 5

Four days ago the temperature was below zero, and today we have a thunder shower! This is a horrible-looking country now: mountains of snow, rivers of water, and acres of bare ground, all in one view. The boys are cutting up the drifts to let the water into the sloughs. There used to be bad floods here, but since so much of the ground is plowed, the water is absorbed. They are shoveling open the drifts in front of the tool house so as to haul out the seeders.

APRIL 21

Spring has jumped right on us. The boys were up early and off. The prairie hens made the air whirr this morning, and a kill-deer sang to me of old times and home. The meadow larks were singing too as I pulled the straw off the peonies in my little seven by nine flower garden. Men can fence a sixty-acre lot for a pasture, but an old woman can have only a twelve-foot garden for posies, which will soon be narrowed to six feet and no flowers at that.

Yesterday I stepped off the kitchen stairs at the side, three steps high. My hands were full, and I could not see my way. I came down with a crash which did not hurt me much at the time, but today I am very lame, my sides ache, I have several black marks, my ankle is swollen, and I am all used up. Walter advises me to take out an accident policy. Fred saw me fall and says I stopped singing when I hit the floor. No sympathy from anybody except Katie.

There was a perfect din of frog music last night. I have never seen so many frogs anywhere as there are here. They leap from the grass in the summertime when I am walking —great, long, frightful-looking things. I love to hear but not see them.

Here you have music well worth the listening,
Goggle-eyed patriarchs, now and again,
Under the golden stars, glowing and glistening,
Drop a bass note or two into the strain.
—*Hearth and Home.*

APRIL 24

The wind has been increasing to a gale. The straw and everything else that can be lifted is flying around the yard, but the ground is too wet for a dust blizzard. I just went out to shake the tablecloth and the wind took me half across the yard before I could haul in my sails. I pity the seeders for the wind has already dried the top of the soil so that the dirt fills their eyes. The hens have blown against the buildings where they sit, unable to move. Walter brought in twenty-two eggs. Now, when I cook, I shall not have to count noses.

APRIL 28

My red, old-fashioned peonies have stuck their pink noses out of the ground. I covered them up last night. I have watched them ever since I was a little girl: in Vermont, in Wisconsin, and now in Dakota Territory where they still thrive. Anything that can live in this cold country should be reverenced. The rose-colored one and the white one are not up yet. I shall see them later.

Walter brought in the first spring flowers. We used to call them windflowers and sometimes pasque flowers and crocuses, but I think they are true anemones. They are a lovely mauve, well-muffled about their throats with a golden frill, for they come early when the air is chill. They have a smell of spring.

I was sick in bed part of the day and Katie had all the cooking to do. Mary can pare potatoes, but if she is not watched she will have them on the stove any time. The other day they were about half cooked when I told her they would be done too soon. She said, "Wull, I pull the fire out." She can wash, but she doesn't know what to do with the clothes when she has rubbed them. If I were strong enough I should much rather do the work myself. I did not know what a boon it was when I was too poor to have a hired girl.

MAY 7

The country is alive with seeders, drags, horses, and men. It is so late that everybody is rustling. There are four plows running here, and two seeders which take every horse on the place, eighteen. The men are now able to seed the mud holes which were too wet when they started. Fred is working with two balky horses which Cousin Daniel bought last summer. He never whips them. He is much more patient with a team than is Walter. Of course he tells them what he thinks of them, and all that, but he doesn't like to see a team abused.

> Fling wide the grain for those who throw
> The clanking shuttle to and fro,
> In the long rows of humming rooms,
> And into ponderous masses wind
> The web, that from a thousand looms,
> Comes forth to clothe mankind.
> —BRYANT, *The Song of the Sower.*

225

Old Nigger-cat has two kittens. We had seven cats last fall, just enough for the seven wives, had they been content with one apiece. There are only three of them alive this spring, for all the cats here have fits. An old gray Tom came here to take up his abode. It is less than a year since the first rat came to this farm, but already they are very numerous, eating potatoes, cabbages, and wheat.

MAY 10

The grass is just beginning to green in some places. Farmers burn off all the old grass in the spring wherever possible. At night we can see grass fires in every direction. How fiercely they must have raged before these prairies were broken. Nothing but the rivers could have stayed their progress. I think, when it was very dry, they would have jumped the Sheyenne.

It is quiet, queer spring weather, cold and dry with northern lights every night. This afternoon we heard a bird singing in the yard which was enough to call us all out, and behold, a finch of some kind was sitting on one of the little alders! He looked like a bull finch, but he might have been a pine finch. Poor birdie! He must have thought this a poor, barren place for birds. The dusk is haunted by meadow larks. I saw one tonight, and how sweetly he sang as he sat perched on top of the granary! He tipped his head and arched his beautiful neck as if in defiance of Dakota cold. He sometimes sings all day, but I have heard very few robins. There is much animation in the song of the lark, but nothing so sweet as the song of the robin.

The wind blows a hurricane. Great clouds of dust are flying through the air. I think our wheat must be firmly rooted or it would surely blow away. If wheat were a dollar a bushel, sure thing, year after year, a man might endure this country for the sake of gain. But he would then lose his own soul, so what would it profit him?

Grimes and Fred have gone to Fargo to get hats and shoes. Walter is busy with the pigs and horses and cows. He found a little new calf at the barn this morning. I am very glad for I had to churn yesterday with half a week's cream. I have been making butter from two last year's cows. I was determined not to buy any. The mother of the calf is a cow that Walter bought dry last fall. We hope she will prove a good one. The rest of the boys started with a load of potatoes which, if the ground is not too hard, they will plant. Our boys are all Irish except John Martin.

Our crews are nearly always Irish, this being an Irish community.

Mrs. Sampson came running over today saying that one of her boys had broken his leg—yesterday. They had splintered it with lath, but he had cried so hard that they had taken off the lath. She wanted some liniment. She said her husband was going for the doctor "if the boy couldn't stand up by noon." Walter went over with her. He says the leg was so badly swollen that he could not tell whether it was broken or not. The Sampsons own a quarter-section of land and sixteen head of cattle, and could afford a doctor.

Twenty-eight degrees above zero. The month of roses is here and not a violet yet. Walter brought me two pansy plants, one white and one nearly black. I am almost afraid to set them out. Our plants are all overgrown in the hotbed. A man just went by with a buffalo coat on. There was ice on the steps and the water in the slough is entirely frozen over. I told Walter to hunt up his skates. I can only think and dream of how it looks down home, there, with the many trees and the yard full of blooms.

Katie and Mr. Green drove over to Sampson's. Mr. Green said the boy needed a doctor, and he should have one if the town had to pay the bill. Katie said the head of the boy's bed was about a foot from the cook stove. If the Lord tempers the wind to the shorn lamb, that may be the cause of the freeze up last night. Anyway, I hope they will move him away from the stove.

JUNE 8

Katie has sown flower seeds. I am so tired of covering the small garden of perennials we have here. Almost nothing is hardy enough for these prairies. I have covered the peonies until they are as large as washtubs. An Irish neighbor came to see them last year when they were in bloom and exclaimed, "My God, my God!" None of the people here had seen a white or a rose-colored one before. I have rosemary, fleur-de-lis, and old man (southernwood).

Cleveland was nominated for president on the sixth, and Thurman for vice president on the seventh at the St. Louis convention.

(I wrote the above in the dark. I am not sure but that it is an improvement.)

JUNE 16

One hundred degrees at 2 P. M. Walter drove to the elevator and from there to Haggart. About half way between, a storm caught him.

It blew and rained and hailed terrifically. The horse became frightened and started to run for the trees. Walter had to get out and tussel with him. Walter was soaked through although he had on a rubber coat. His linen hat hung in ruffles. We expected to catch it here, but the storm went by to the north of us with only a few drops of rain and a gale of wind. We have many such storms which always come up very suddenly. Walter was only four miles away, soaked to the skin, while Fred was lugging water, here, to wet the cabbages.

The wind whipped off every one of my red peony buds after I had covered them every night for two months. The white and rose were not large enough to snap off, but I fear their time will come. The cabbages will have to be reset. We have to cover to save from frost until it is necessary to cover from the hot sun and wind, and then, in September, begin on the frost again. Fred put on the screens, for the mosquitoes were putting in their bills and the air is full of flies. The boys made a smudge around the house and barns. The cows fairly bellow in their torment.

JUNE 29

A Mr. Fenn came to the farm today. He is a theological student recently from New York

State who is trying to organize a Sabbath school among us heathen. I do not think he will succeed as nearly all the families with children in the neighborhood are Catholics, and it is difficult for Catholics and Protestants to have any unison. He said that if he could secure Katie for superintendent he would organize at once, for he had the consent of the school board to use the schoolhouse. No man seems willing to take it in hand, and Katie doesn't like to. Mr. Fenn is to stay with us tonight and visit the people tomorrow. He is a quiet little gentleman, and praised my bread.

The Republicans have nominated Harrison for president and Morton for vice-president. Now, I presume we will get some Tippecanoe in it, of which I heard so much in my grandfather's time. Right here I shall bet my bottom dollar that they will not be elected.

JULY 4

A bright, windy morning ushers in the glorious Fourth, although it is unusually quiet on the prairie and seems like Sunday. We hear a distant boom, but whether it is the cannon or the thunder which promises the Fourth of July storm that is nearly always on hand, I cannot say. All the boys, except Walter, have gone to Fargo. There is no celebration there but they must go somewhere. There is a picnic, a Norwegian affair, down on the Sheyenne where there are some lovely places. Katie and Walter and I have been alone at our meals, which seemed so strange that we couldn't eat anything.

Two men came here today, one a possible buyer, the other a Fargo boomer who said, " 'Tis the best country in God's world." About next Christmas the man will see, if he buys. He is from Baltimore and wants the farm for his son. He seemed well pleased with it.

Harry has bought a farm sixty miles from here—a very large farm consisting of five sections of land, well stocked, with good buildings on it. The name of the place is Eckleson. He went there today. We shall be lonesome without him. He was our first caller when we came here six years ago, and he has been a regular one since—whenever Katie is at home.

JULY 10

Yesterday our cat caught a bird, a meadow lark that was sitting close by. We have watched her from the first until her eggs were nearly ready to hatch. I could have killed old Nig! This morning the bird's mate was singing, not in a joyous strain as usual, but plaintively as one could readily understand. Maybe he thinks she has deserted him and her nest, but he can never call her back. I am a lover of birds and my name is enrolled in the Audubon Society.

Walter went to Fargo to find a girl and came back with a French woman, Mary Magdalene, about fifty years old. She, poor thing, is poverty stricken and has left a farm to come here and earn four dollars a week.

The boys in the hayfield are suffering today with the temperature at 104 degrees. Poor Dan looks like a gray horse instead of the milk-white steed that he actually is. I suppose he is old but he is always fat and handsome. How I shall hate to part with our horses! I love them all.

We made no fire for tea. Fred came in, warm, and said, "Give us a hand-out." I gave them raised biscuits, cold beef and potatoes, jelly, and iced milk. Some of the school children stopped here today completely exhausted from the heat. They walk two miles.

JULY 14

Our men are in the hay field. There is a large amount of hay down which must be put into the barns before harvest. Elsie cut all the forenoon, down in their big hay field alone. What would people think in Kingston, I wonder, if a girl should go to Marquette with a mower to cut hay all day! Sometimes her sister, Lena, rakes. They have hauled home five loads apiece from the hay field, making thirty-five miles each. Elsie weighs 104 pounds. They have a man to pitch the hay on, and the girls build the load, haul it home, and pitch it off onto the stack which their father and mother build. Such people can make a living in Dakota. They had only eighteen dollars in the world to start on. They took up land here, and now own two quarter-sections; have horses, cattle, sheep, trees, shrubs, a flower garden,—and eight young ones. Most of the settlers spread round and rode in their carriages while wheat was $1.50 a bushel, and when it went down, mortgaged their farms.

JULY 17

I am cooking beet greens with my beef and pork. I pulled a bushel. We have only ten in the family but the three new ones are very heavy eaters, the woman ahead.

We have had some hard showers with the rain coming in torrents. I never saw it rain so hard. The mosquitoes are very troublesome, crawling through the screens and coming in on people's clothes. Not many get into the front room nor the chambers. We can see smudges rising all around the prairie. Mary filled the stove with green hay and nearly killed everybody in the house. Whether it killed the mosquitoes, I am uncertain. Katie asked her today to blacken the stove, but she said, "Dat's a man's work." There is not a man on the farm with so brawny an arm as hers.

JULY 20

The mercury was 104 at 2 P. M. Walter came in for a drink, purple in the face, the sweat pouring from him cutting streaks and gutters through the dirt on his face. The hay in the slough is very dusty, and the men came in at seven for supper looking like black men. Today is the last day of school. There is now a month's vacation, then three months more of school.

JULY 22, SUNDAY

Katie, Walter, and Fred started for Sabbath school. Finally all the boys went, saying they were going for the purpose of quelling any disturbance which might arise. Last Sabbath a young man who worked in the neighborhood cracked parlor matches under his heels, laughed aloud, and talked so that he disturbed the school. None of the men said anything to him, so Katie asked him to leave, which he did. He came again this Sabbath to have more fun, but when he saw that the crowd was against him, he left without going inside.

The hired men said they had the boxing gloves in the wagon as they didn't want to kill him.

My dog, Jack, killed three big rats this morning. He is the most determined dog I ever saw. He will tear down a building to get at a rat. He and McAuliffe's dog recently went visiting at the same place. Jack thought it best to send McAuliffe's dog home which was no easy matter. So they fought until Jack killed him. I was very sorry, and I expect he will be killed himself some time for one of the hasty things he does.

JULY 28

The temperature was 100 at 3 P. M. and Katie and I nearly melted at our work, but we have to prepare three meals a day no matter what happens. The fog drifted early, as the sun struggled through, and hung on the window screens in beads. It is unhealthy weather: cold fog in the morning and hot enough to boil one's blood later on.

I suppose this is my last summer on this farm, and no doubt it is the last summer that I shall have anyone who needs or wants me. I had hoped never to see that time, but I have come to it. Had it not been for Cousin Daniel's farm, the time would have come sooner than this—I mean the time of the breaking up of the family. We could not all have stayed at home in Kingston these last six years. No letters today from Daniel nor Nellie nor Theron, the three that comprise my outside world.

JULY 30

This morning at five the sky looked so fearful that I thought we were going to have a cyclone. The black clouds flew, the lightning flashed, and the thunder roared, but the greater part of the storm went to the south of us, down to South Dakota where they so often get the worst of it.

A new man came today and started plowing with a walking plow. The boys said they saw him in Fargo in a drunken condition, so I presume he is dead broke and obliged to come into the country to work. He looks as though work would come hard. The country is full of such men in summer and fall who work like slaves and then leave every cent in the saloons. I feel sorry for them. Many a drunkard has expended more virtue in a vain endeavor to break his chains than suffices to carry an ordinary Christian to heaven.

AUGUST 1

The weather has been wet and foggy and disagreeable. Everything drips with dampness. Fred wears rubber boots every morning when he milks the cows. This morning the fog was so dense that we could see nothing at all. Now, it is coming off hot and I am afraid the wheat will be mildewed. We are having entirely too much rain, but who's to stop it? Steve and Dominic and Buckskin Jim are plowing. John Grimes quit work. He was no rustler. I fed one great tramp. The country is full of them. Many are not regular tramps, but men hunting work who have come too soon—before the harvest is ready. The Waltz boys came from Kingston to work through harvest.

We make fourteen pounds of butter a week from three cows. I have one hundred pounds already packed for harvest. I wonder if anybody was ever before tired enough to be sick at his stomach. I have been for the past three nights. When I become rested I get over it. Katie baked a half bushel of cookies yesterday while I was resting. We now have no help with the cooking. I might as well have my feet ache as my soul tried by the help we get, and they must all have four dollars a week for trying us. Walter has gone repeatedly to the intelligence office in Fargo, but only the poorest girls apply to the office for places. The other day he heard of one in Moorhead, drove there, and found a Swedish girl, just over, who could not speak one word of English. He has very little time to run around the country looking for girls.

Two degrees above freezing with no wind. We all shivered round until the sun was two hours high. The boys have been working on the road with a grader. Never were there seen five better looking horses than started out with it today. They are fixing the machinery, grinding the sickles, and cleaning and oiling the reapers—getting ready for harvest.

Walter has been quite lame through his back and stomach. He drove his team up to the machine where the boys were grinding feed to see if the horses would be afraid. He found himself left very quickly. The team went flying through the wheat fields, and he lamed himself trying to hang on to them. I have physicked him and plastered mustard all over his stomach.

I was up betimes starting in the new girl that Walter brought yesterday. She is a Norwegian girl named Tilda Olson. She cannot talk much English, but she looks right. She is strong and clean, although she may not be used to our ways. I cannot understand anything she says but she explains that she can "feestan" me.

About nine o'clock last night Katie said, "Hark, didn't someone rap?" A caller is such an unusual thing on the prairie at that hour that Walter did not hesitate to yell, "Come in!" when, to his amazement, in walked the minister, Mr. Fenn. He came out to visit the school but did not get there in time. Walter cared for his horse, and we got him supper and bed. Mr. Fenn is a fine little gentleman, who has traveled in Dakota all summer organizing Sabbath schools and selling papers, Bibles, and other books. He is also an amateur photographer, carrying his apparatus with him. Before he left today he took a picture of the house, Katie, Fred, Jack, and his own pony and carriage—a group picture, all on one plate.

AUGUST 19, SUNDAY

All men harvesting. There is too great a risk to wheat to let it go on the Sabbath day—risk from hail, wind, and rain storms. Yesterday there was a hard white frost. The clothes on the grass froze stiff. The last frost was on June second—that leaves us July free from frost. What a fruit country this would be! Oh, dear, the corn, cucumbers, flowers, and potatoes are black in the garden! We had a handsome garden which was the admiration of all who saw it. We had just one mess of cucumbers and no corn or beans, and now everything that the frost will kill is dead. The greatest loss is, of course, the eight acres of potatoes which had the best of care. They lie now, a great black mass, not half grown. They were later than those in the garden which we have been using.

The frost must have injured the wheat that was backward, but we think ours was all out of the way. The harvesters are doing good work, fast, and Fred, who is shocking, says it is the best and cleanest wheat we have had on the farm. The men made twelve miles cutting yesterday afternoon on this section.

AUGUST 25

The men have suffered with the heat in the fields today. They have drunk gallons of ice water. My vines lie black and dead before the wheat is in the stack. Walter found another new calf at the barn this morning, a Hereford, a nice one too. The mother cow grew rapidly worse and died at noon. I think she had puerperal fever. We gave her everything we could think of to save her; nitre oil, salts, linseed tea, and poulticed her bag with bran, salt, and flaxseed. She groaned like a human being all the time. Walter and Jim skinned her and drew her off after dark. The poor little motherless calf is doing well on new milk. There is also a new litter of nine speckled pigs.

Many people say our wheat is the best in

Cass County; however, Walter thinks the frost injured it where it was the greenest. It has stayed in the milk too long. The report is that the crop is about half ruined; some of it by hot, dry winds which prevailed about the Fourth of July, and some by frost when it was in the milk which shrunk it. Many farmers are plowing under their grain, or cutting it for feed, or burning it. Ours is a good yield and splendid wheat. Thanks!

I fully expected to see Cousin Daniel tonight. I feel sure he is on his way, and I find myself watching for him even with the spyglass.

AUGUST 28

Dakota is different in many ways from the country down east. Nobody keeps track of his neighbors here. People come and go; families move in and out, and nobody asks whence they came nor whither they go. Walter went down to see if he could get water from a flowing well a mile and a half from here, and found that the owner of the farm had died last winter. I have lived here six years and I do not know who occupies half of the surrounding farms although they are in full view.

The boys finished cutting wheat yesterday. Walter went to Fargo after a crew. He came back with three men and one team, but he said there were nine more men and two more teams on the road. We waited up for them until ten o'clock when three of them came saying they had gotten lost but had seen a light and followed it here. The other men with the teams camped all night beside a hay stack. All the men reached here this morning in time for breakfast. Walter had gotten up early and butchered a hog, and I fried the liver for breakfast. We now have twenty-five men, among them Tom Carney, the engineer, and Mr. Melon, the fireman. We have the same old cook who got in running order in time to get dinner and took sixteen men out with him.

AUGUST 30

A regular procession started for the quarter-section after dinner: engine, which is a motor, ahead; teams all behind, eleven of them. Fred hauled the first load this year. The population of Dakota must now be immense. I can see a dozen threshing machines from here and the smoke of as many more. I think wheat will rise in price, for there is a shortage everywhere, so the papers say. We have hoped for that change for six years and now that we are about ready to leave, it has come.

It doesn't seem possible that we have been here so long—here where the summers come and go so rapidly that one can scarcely keep track of time. This is a most uncertain country for crops. This year we escaped drought and hail but frost cut the wheat crop the last thing. Harry writes that only half of his 1,-400 acres will pay for the harvesting and he will not cut all the grain. This will be a great loss as he had depended on money obtained from this crop to make a payment on his new farm.

SEPTEMBER 2, SUNDAY

All threshing. There is no Sunday in Dakota. I have blistered my toes since the threshers came. The cook keeps food in the store room and in the refrigerator at the house, and I keep trotting to wait on him. Tilda is willing but she cannot understand what he wants. Walter flies from the machine to the blacksmith shop. Today, I thought his team was running away. He is quite an expert at the blacksmith trade now.

SEPTEMBER 8

The men threshed 1,300 bushels, but finally had to stop for the wind blew so hard that they could not keep the belt on the machine. It blew the bundles, too, so that they could not manage them, which often happens in Dakota. The men lie around the yard, playing ball, resting, and washing their clothes. It is very trying to have threshers on the place. Everything is upset. Pails, lanterns, and all things movable are missing. These men have gotten along very well together. We had thirty men at one time and there was not a cross word nor a quarrel all through.

Cousin Daniel arrived at the farm looking well although thinner than he was last year. I am afraid he has come too late for the climate to improve his health. I seldom see such an old-time friend as he. He reminds me of many things that passed long ago when we were both young. The chances of selling the farm appear to be poor after the injury by frost which the crops have suffered. Daniel and Walter have been taking inventory. Daniel feels rather tired and sleepy and not like stirring around much yet. He laughed to think I was watching for him when he was in Vermont on the other side of the Green Mountains.

SEPTEMBER 10

A still, lovely day with a grand mirage. Harry took Katie to Fargo. The weather was so pleasant that I thought the ride would do her good and I knew it would Harry. The threshing was finished at twelve, noon, and most of the men left as soon as Walter made out their time. Everybody is glad. It seems like a calm after a storm. Picking up after threshers indoors and out is an endless task. Tilda is washing the men's bedding and she has a lively lot of clothes. If we can manage to keep the house free from these insects we are thankful.

SEPTEMBER 16

Sunday, and how different from last Sabbath! Then, the threshers were here and all was bustle and confusion; today, all is peaceful and quiet and as a Sabbath day should be.

The inventory is finished and Daniel has $6,000 in personal property alone. No poor man can buy him out, and no rich man wants to with wheat so low. I think he will have to lease his farm, as he will not operate it longer.

SEPTEMBER 19

Last night after I was ready for bed, I went out to see if Roxy had water and to give her a few pats as usual, but her box was empty. Nobody knew when she went out and as she is so helpless I had little hope of finding her. I got Walter up and we hunted for an hour. Finally we heard a faint cry, followed it, and found her way out in the middle of Griffin's quarter-section. I was very glad to get her back.

I was sick all day. Tonight I have gotten

up into Fred's bedroom over the store room where a red hot chimney goes through. From having a chill, I now have to go downstairs again with a fever.

SEPTEMBER 23, SUNDAY

I feel somewhat better. Katie is a capital nurse and cooled my fever. She did my head in cold cloths, my feet in cabbage leaves, made me sage tea and crust coffee, gave me a Dover's powder, and is now giving me rhubarb and soda. She knows how to do everything correctly but she has not the strength to do hard work.

Harry came this morning and wanted Katie to ride over to his sister's with him. I have been alone all day with the exception of Tilda who makes no progress in speaking English. Today is warm and pleasant and sunshiny and I have been out sunning myself, but my fever comes on at evening and will last until midnight.

SEPTEMBER 27

Two of our boys who have often disagreed flew at each other today in the barn and had a regular fist fight. Katie saw them fighting and called Walter who put a stop to it, although Fred would like to have seen them fight to a finish. Jim Markham went to the field and plowed awhile, but concluded that if he stayed Dutch Henry would not give up the feud, so he left. Walter hired the first man who came along as we cannot afford to have a plow lie idle. The new man's name is Johnson and he is Swedish, at least his fleece is white as snow.

I saw a flock of little birds in my flower garden just at night. I think they are birds of passage for I have never seen them in winter. They will soon be gone.

> Oh, haste little birdie to some warmer clime,
> The wind whistles o'er the bleak wold,
> The stubble is brown and all seared with the rime,
> Fierce winter is coming, so cold!
> —Self.

OCTOBER 2

Pleasant all day and warm and yellow; however, it froze quite hard last night and there was ice around the door this morning. Katie and Walter came from Fargo without any wraps, although they wore their astrakhan coats down. Katie bought a new dress and some other things. They brought a letter from Daniel who had arrived safely; and a book from Theron, one of his own publications.

Roxy was lost again today. Walter went to hunt for her with a horse and buggy and found her about a mile from home, all tired out. The plow boys had heard her cry and had taken her up. When I let her out I watch un-

Fred Woodward

Seeders at Work, Grain Elevator in Background

Harry W. Green

Early Fargo

til she comes in, but Tilda will let her out and I do not know it until she is gone. I hunt her up every day and am constantly looking after her. Although she is deaf and blind, I think she has the sense of smell which took her toward the plow teams. Poor Roxy, who never did a bit of harm in all her sixteen years of life!

OCTOBER 8

Yesterday Katie started for Wisconsin, and one long day has passed without her. It seems that she will be home now, tonight, but many a long, dreary night must pass before I see her again. I could never have let her go except for the hope of improving her health. I am alone, for it amounts to that. Tilda cannot talk to me; Walter, the reader, will sit here a whole evening absorbed in his book; and Fred will not sit here at all if he can help it. But I should not feel discouraged for Katie will enjoy herself with Nellie and the children and I am glad she is there.

OCTOBER 10

Every morning teams string by to Fargo with the grain. The small farmers haul their wheat to the mill where they receive one dollar a bushel for No. 1 hard. There is very little of that grade in the country this year. Walter has made a rack or crib in which to haul straw. The men pile such huge loads on it that we were almost frightened the first time they drove it into the yard.

The boys killed an immense hog which weighed 457 pounds. It was fattened altogether on screenings. We have thirty hogs and pigs and it is quite a task to feed them. The screenings are ground and kept soaking in barrels in winter, but fed dry in summer. Pork is fourteen cents a pound. Now, here is a market for shrunken wheat.

## OCTOBER 16

Two months ago everything froze to death, and today there was a thunder shower. I have been piecing a comfortable of some old black and red cashmere. It was all spread out on the front room floor when in came Harry, who I supposed was in Eckleson. I seemed to see Katie on the instant—really to see her—and I was so confused that I hardly knew what to say to him. She has been gone a week—one long week. I get along very well days, but the nights are endless, and I hear every little noise. The gnawing of a mouse kept me awake last night which it does not do when Katie is in bed with me, though it often does her.

## OCTOBER 19

Twenty this morning. The air was filled with frost, the sun shining through it with a soft light like a lantern in a fog. The weeds and stubble resembled marabou feathers. The short, curly prairie grass looked as if the earth had powdered her bangs. The frost stayed on until eight o'clock.

The teams started for the elevator—four-horse teams, three with grain boxes and one with a double wagon box—Walter ahead with the buggy. Quite a procession! Before they were halfway there the rain began, and, although they had canvas to cover the wheat, they themselves became very wet. Thus ended the first day's wheat hauling. I suppose this is the last farming Walter will do on the Dodge farm, so he wants to haul off all the wheat. The railroad companies are not putting cars on the sidetracks for the farmers this year as has been done heretofore. We have always shipped the wheat and saved the elevator charges.

Wheat is a dollar again; it was ninety cents last week. We think about half of ours is No. 1 hard. A great deal of it is graded No. 1 northern now, which does not bring as much; then there is No. 2 northern and rejected, which bring less.

NOVEMBER 2

Dominic came back today to settle and pack. He will go to Kingston. That is the only place I can think of as home, although when I do

251

get there it will not be home to me without my children. Fred has been away a week visiting Harry's farm. I thought surely he would be on the Jimtown train but he was not. It has rained and hailed and snowed and is gloomy and lonesome. The sky looks like a ledge of rock, but I am not afraid it will fall. The weather has been dark almost constantly since Katie went away.

Walter took Tilda to Fargo. I commenced doing the work by washing the empty jars, pans, pails, and jugs which a hired girl always leaves dirty until she needs them. The last man has gone. It seems queer, indeed, to have only one man in the family. Roxy and I are alone down stairs. She is a great deal of company for me as I get up with her every night.

NOVEMBER 5

Fred returned this morning bringing three wild geese. He said he shot a dozen while there, close to Harry's farm. I have picked two and sent one to a neighbor.

Later. I cooked a goose for dinner. Roxy smelled it and came into the kitchen teasing for some. The boys had come in for dinner when suddenly I realized that she was not there. I began searching for her at once. I soon saw Jack in the cow pasture barking at the cow and calf which was unusual. I hurried there and found poor Roxy just dying. The cow had hooked her to death. I was too faint to bring her in, and she was dead when Fred got there. Oh, how I did cry! I have taken care of her for sixteen years and I shall miss her very much.

I slept very little last night for I could not keep Roxy out of my mind. What a terrible ending to her life! She knew everything and never did a mean thing. I have had her sleep by me since Katie went away. Last night I imagined I heard the patter of her feet; then I would wake and think how tragic it was for that beast to toss her to death. She lies in her box in the tool house covered with her blanket. Jack teased me all the evening to bring her in. He would whine at the door and, as soon as it was opened, would hurry out where she lay. He stayed there beside her all night.

I suppose the whole country is in a fever of excitement. Fred has gone to Mapleton to election. He wishes he were out of the territory so that he could vote for Cleveland. The liquor license question is the greatest subject of controversy here now.

A foggy, dark morning. Fred came home at noon. He is constable and worked at the polls, and went to Fargo with the ballot. He sat up all night watching the bulletins. When he came away Cleveland and Harrison were even, or nearly so. Of course, the Democrats said Cleveland was ahead, and the Republicans, Harrison.

Walter and Fred dug a grave out by the granary and buried poor Roxy. Walter put a cover on the box in which she always slept and in it she will lie as long as she is turning to dust. I should be glad she were gone if she had not met such a terrible end. I have looked after her for so many years, and then I was not there to defend her in her great need, and she, blind and deaf. I should have watched her more carefully, but it was almost impossible when I was doing the work, and I never thought of the cow's hurting her. I suppose in her blind way she went near the calf. Jack teased us to bring Roxy in all the time until she was buried. When we took him out to the tool house where she lay, he would pull the blanket and whine. Now he sits out by her grave. The cow has bawled all day for her calf which I was glad to hear. I cried when she killed my Roxy.

NOVEMBER 10

Just as we were sitting down to dinner Mr. and Mrs. Ballard came. She wished to see the place where she will live for a few years at least. She has a baby three months old, very pretty and sweet; an only child.

Walter and Fred are out around the yard fixing up things for winter, perhaps our last in this cold region. They have been in only to their meals, but I am content as long as they are near. This is the coldest night we have had this fall. The wind sounds dismal as it whistles around the house; and as the creak of the swinging clothes reel reaches my ears, I fancy I hear poor Roxy cry. Jack now sleeps in the house.

NOVEMBER 16

The Fort Yates man who stopped here last April came along again today on his way back to the Fort. He stays all night, and is entertaining the boys with his experiences with the Indians at Standing Rock Agency, where he lives right among them. He has on a long, blue Army overcoat, a buckskin coat under it, and a raccoonskin cap. He travels in an old covered wagon. He has pigs inside it and a splendid Polled Angus bull, which he is taking home, tied on behind. All together they are unique.

NOVEMBER 17

The immigrant wagon started west this morning, the man having rested himself, and his bull, his pigs, and his horses. He has almost two hundred miles to go with poor horses. The boys were interested in his stories of the western country around the Missouri River, for they expect to go farther west some day. He told how the men of the Agency would start out with about 2,500 Indians on a buffalo hunt. Sometimes in one expedition they killed as many as 4,000 buffaloes. No wonder that animal is rapidly disappearing.[1]

NOVEMBER 26

A beautiful, warm day and nearly four months ago everything froze, even the wheat crop. Walter's birthday. He received three white silk handkerchiefs with his initials nicely embroidered from a lady in Oconomowoc. They are beautiful but her love is nothing as compared to mine. He has never had a rival in my affections.

I had been hoping for good weather so that Katie might arrive in safety. She came today. Walter found her at the Headquarters Hotel and they returned to the farm at one o'clock. Now, let it storm!

---

[1] As late as 1882 large herds of buffaloes roamed the Western prairies, and about that time the last great slaughter of the animals took place. Professional hunters came to the Territory, and hunts were carried on and products shipped under contract. Practically all the early settlers earned money picking bones from the prairies and shipping them out at $8 and $10 a ton. In 1884 one newspaper reported 100 tons shipped for that season. Hides brought from $1.25 to $3.25 apiece, and were sent east to be made into robes and coats.

Thanksgiving. Walter, Katie, Fred, and I are together. So few to do for! but they are those I love and I shall, as I have always done, give them a good dinner.

We have had our roast duck, cranberry sauce, and fruit cake, and are as happy as we could be without the rest of the family. Harry Green came this evening. He has not been here for several weeks, but *happened* to come soon after Katie returned.

The fall has been so long and warm and dry that the farmers will have no excuse if their fall plowing is not done. The country looks black and dreary now that so much soil is turned over. Prairie fires are growing few in spite of the fact that the sloughs are full of dried grass, weeds, daisies, sunflowers, and other coarse vegetation which make a terrific fire. The fire follows the course of the sloughs for miles and miles and lights up the whole country. I love to watch it.

> Alone the Fire, when frost-winds sere
> The heavy herbage of the ground,
> Gathers his annual harvest here,
> With roaring like the battle's sound.
> —BRYANT, *The Hunter of the Prairies.*

257

Elsie Lessing came here to make a dress for her grandmother so as to keep it a secret from her father. The old lady is Mrs. Lessing's mother who lives in Wisconsin. Although Mrs. Lessing and Elsie have carried on the work of the farm and bought the goods with their own money, they dare not let Mr. Lessing know of the plan. There are not many such scamps in the world as he. Elsie is in need of many things, yet she denies herself to make her grandmother a present.

Just zero at 3 P. M. It looks wintry with everything covered with snow. The boys are putting away tools and harnesses so that nothing will be left under the snow when we have the auction in March. This is Fred's birthday. It doesn't seem possible that he is twenty-four for he is just as much a boy as ever. Katie and I washed, melting the ice yesterday which means a cold for both of us.

Another dark day with the wind blowing from the south—a Wisconsin day, Walter calls it. I read of a blizzard east on the St. Lawrence; and in Canada they seem to have the start of us this time. This is the warmest November and December we have ever known in Dakota.

I made a fire in the back kitchen and

scrubbed the floors. They get very muddy. A little snow, just enough to stick the mud to the feet, is a fearful thing in this black gummy soil.

> With mud and with grime from corner to center,
> Forever at war and forever alert,
> No rest for a day lest the evening enter;
> I've spent my whole life in a struggle with dirt.

DECEMBER 24

It is Christmas Eve and I am thinking of the merry times we used to have, all of us at home on this night, many years ago. The happiest part was when the children hung their stockings in a long row on the mantelpiece. Their father always saw that they were filled with good things such as candy and nuts, whatever else they received.

> There's a song in the air!
> There's a star in the sky!
> There's a mother's deep prayer
> And a baby's low cry!
> And the star rains its fire while the Beautiful
>   sing,
> And the manger of Bethlehem cradles a king.
>         —L. G. HOLLAND, *A Christmas Carol.*

DECEMBER 25

A bright, peaceful Christmas morning with a beautiful mirage. I have been wishing that Christmas bells could ring out on the prairies on this clear, shining day. But they can be heard only in imagination. The boys brought Katie a pair of fine silk stockings and a Wirt fountain pen. Fred gave Walter Dante's *Inferno* for a Christmas present. The book is beautifully bound in morocco, but oh, the illustrations are horrible! They make me shudder. Katie presented me with a candlestick and Elsie Lessing brought us a cup and saucer.

DECEMBER 30, SUNDAY

This is the last Sabbath of 1888 and a very pleasant one. About eleven o'clock Fred brought his old girl, Evaline, from Fargo where he had gone to meet her. I was surprised to learn that the trains were late yesterday because of snow. Evaline was told that the cars would not connect, so she stayed with friends in Minneapolis until yesterday morning's train. The six years that have passed since we left Kingston have transformed her from a little girl into a young lady, and a very pretty one, too.

DECEMBER 31

Another year is dying fast,
A checkered year of joy and woe,
And dark and light alike are past,
The rose and thorn at once laid low.

This is the last entry in this diary. Very soon the year 1888 will have passed into history. But if it were not for the end of the year, where would we find time to make new resolutions, to swear off from old vices, and to commence on a new plan? It is a sort of fetching up place. The shadows lengthen as the night draws near, and with the advent of another day a new year will be born.

> Good-bye, Old Year, with your white drawn face,
> Your chaste and saddened past;
> Into your place with swift, proud step,
> The Young Year glides at last.

IN THE SPRING of 1889 the Woodward family, all except Katie, left Dakota forever. She was to return three years later as the wife of Harry Green, and they were to live many years on his own bonanza farm purchased in that far-off time. The family returned to the old brown house in Kingston, Wisconsin. They repaired and remodeled it; they raked the yard, trimmed the trees, and made garden. A new coal stove was set up, and there was water close to the door and wood in the back kitchen.

That summer Walter married Carrie Howard, "the lady from Oconomowoc" of the diary, and they went to make a home in Two Harbors, Minnesota, where they still reside. They took Fred with them to help with the business, so that at last Mary Dodge Woodward and Katie were all that were left in the old home. For Katie, there were Harry's letters from Dakota; the G. A. R. Basket Festival at the hotel; Children's Day at the church; the dance in Vince's Hall; Uncle Tom's Cabin; and the band convention still talked about in that reminiscent village when four bands paraded the streets and then went to the grove and played two hours, after which there was a "ball play" with the Kingston boys playing the Markesans.

They made nightshirts for Theron; they made pieced quilts; and Mary made a crazy foot quilt, the last work of her tired hands. There were the letters to and visits from the children. There was the work in the little garden where had been raised sixteen different kinds of fruits and vegetables besides flowers innumerable. But a little weeding or hoeing now made Mary's head reel and her back ache.

Then, in the late summer, when many of the flowers she loved were laying their tired heads on the breast of the cooling earth to take their long rest, Mary Dodge Woodward fell ill. It might have been the effects of the spring sprouting of the potatoes in the cellar, or the work in the garden, or the aftermath of la grippe which had everyone in its throes that year. Her dear old friend Dr. Lawn was called in and pronounced the ailment lung fever. Telegrams now whizzed back and forth; Theron sent wine and grapes, oranges, bananas, peaches, and boxes of California preserved fruits. Mr. Olmstead, the minister, called and offered a prayer for her restoration to health. One by one the family came home until they were all there—all five of them—

a silent, sad-faced group, with Ma too sick to visit much.

Much of her life through the checkered years must have passed before her eyes as in review, as she lay there dying, aware of all that went on around her, solicitous for their comforts, trying to dispel their anxieties, tired and weak but cheerful still. On Christmas Eve they knew that her life was drawing quietly toward its close, and on December 25, 1890, she passed peacefully away.